Early praise for *Test-Driven React*

Test-Driven React is a great hands-on introduction to the latest technologies in front-end development. Even if you have little experience with React and front-end testing, the detailed examples in this book will guide you every step of the way to creating working and tested code.

➤ **Ludovico Fischer**
  Author of *React for Real*

This book is an amazing timesaver for those entering the world of modern Java-Script. It's full of tips for the whole React development ecosystem, including VS Code, Jest, Babel, ESLint, Webpack, Enzyme, and many other tools. I'm sure that most developers, even those already quite experienced, should find it more than worthwhile.

➤ **Stefan Turalski**
  FX Software Developer, BNP Paribas

Twenty-first century web app development (especially in React) can easily become a morass of npm dependencies, copy-pasted Stack Overflow code, and general kludginess. Fortunately, there is hope, in the shape of test-driven development (TDD): write a failing test; make it pass; refactor; repeat. Trevor Burnham's *Test-Driven React* will help lead you back from the brink so you can make web development pleasurable again.

➤ **Richard Murnane**
  Software Developer, 3P Learning

JavaScript development can sometimes feel overwhelming: so many different frameworks, so much configuration. You don't always know where to start. *Test-Driven React* cuts straight through all the confusion, and quickly gets you on the path to shoring up your React apps with solid test coverage. And the techniques Trevor provides extend even beyond React. I'm certain I'll be referring to this book for all my future JavaScript projects.

➤ **Darin Wilson**
   Principal Software Engineer, Infinite Red

Test-Driven React will be a most trusted companion for anyone eager for professional and battle-tested practices applied to the React ecosystem. If you want to learn how to develop robust, safe and maintainable applications, this is the way to go.

➤ **Peter Perlepes**
   Lead Front-Line Engineer, Welcome Pickups

This is an incredibly comprehensive guide to improving the testing and development workflows of React developers at any experience level. Whether you're looking to test a React component for the first time or rework your testing workflow after years in the industry, *Test Driven React*'s engaging and interactive lessons will fundamentally change how you think about JavaScript testing.

➤ **Adam Markon**
   Software Engineer, HubSpot

In an era when big structures are built with small components, unit tests and TDD are a must for every React developer.

➤ **Tim Givois**
   Senior Engineer, Wizeline

Test-Driven React

Find Problems Early, Fix Them Quickly, Code with Confidence

Trevor Burnham

The Pragmatic Bookshelf

Raleigh, North Carolina

Many of the designations used by manufacturers and sellers to distinguish their products are claimed as trademarks. Where those designations appear in this book, and The Pragmatic Programmers, LLC was aware of a trademark claim, the designations have been printed in initial capital letters or in all capitals. The Pragmatic Starter Kit, The Pragmatic Programmer, Pragmatic Programming, Pragmatic Bookshelf, PragProg and the linking *g* device are trademarks of The Pragmatic Programmers, LLC.

Every precaution was taken in the preparation of this book. However, the publisher assumes no responsibility for errors or omissions, or for damages that may result from the use of information (including program listings) contained herein.

Our Pragmatic books, screencasts, and audio books can help you and your team create better software and have more fun. Visit us at *https://pragprog.com*.

The team that produced this book includes:

Publisher: Andy Hunt
VP of Operations: Janet Furlow
Managing Editor: Susan Conant
Development Editor: Jacquelyn Carter
Copy Editor: Jasmine Kwityn
Indexing: Potomac Indexing, LLC
Layout: Gilson Graphics

For sales, volume licensing, and support, please contact *support@pragprog.com*.

For international rights, please contact *rights@pragprog.com*.

ISBN-13: 978-1-68050-646-4
Book version: P1.0—June 2019

Contents

Acknowledgments

This book wouldn't have been possible without the help of many people. The lion's share of the thanks belongs to my editor at the Pragmatic Bookshelf, Jackie Carter, for pushing this project forward. Thanks to everyone who took the time to do technical review: Ludovico Fischer, Tim Givois, Adam Markon, Julie Nergararian, Peter Perlepes, and Stefan Turalski. Thanks as well to everyone who reported errata during the beta, including John Paul Ashenfelter, Matthew Boynes, Nehemiah Burian, Charles Hoffman, Bob Kuo, Jessica Lawrence, Douglas Lovell, Jason Meridth, Richard Murnane, and Philip Westwell.

Further thanks are due to the whole Pragmatic Bookshelf team, and to my fellow authors who provided support. This is my fourth book written under their banner. Although the process is invariably governed by Hofstadter's Law,[1] I've found writing for the Pragmatic Bookshelf immeasurably rewarding.

Last but not least, thanks to my darling Tooky Kavanagh. You mean the world to me.

---

1. https://en.wikipedia.org/wiki/Hofstadter%27s_law

Introduction

I vividly remember the first time I wrote code. I was 10 years old and utterly obsessed with robots. The local public library must have lent me every book they had on the subject. One of those books had an appendix: "Write Your Own Robot in BASIC." I ran to my parents' computer, fired up qbasic (bundled with the cutting-edge MS-DOS operating system), and fed in the instructions for my robot companion.

The program was unimpressive by today's standards. It was a primitive version of what we would now call a "chatbot." It would give you a prompt like

```
>>> Greetings, human. How are you feeling today?
```

then wait for you to enter a recognizable string like tired, and give an appropriate response like

```
>>> I am sorry to hear that. How about a nice cup of coffee?
```

and so on. The only keywords in the entire program were IF, THEN, and GOTO.

Even though my chatbot wouldn't stand a snowball's chance in a Turing test, the exercise was a revelation to me: I could actually *create* something just by *typing*. Now it seemed that robots were old news. Computers were where it's at!

As computers have grown more capable, software has grown more complex, and that thrilling feeling has become more elusive. New layers of abstraction have empowered me to do more with less code, but at the cost of constant uncertainty: *Will my code do what I intended?*

Test-driven development (TDD) is the art of minimizing that uncertainty, allowing you to feel confident about your code from the moment you write it. How? By making a few assertions about that code beforehand. This groundwork sets up a short, satisfying feedback loop: as soon as you write your code, the tests light up green. Afterward, the tests remain in place, standing guard against regressions.

I don't always use TDD, but when I do, I feel a little bit closer to the magic of that first coding experience. All of the rigamarole of modern software development fades away. I can focus all my energies on reaching toward the green light.

What's in This Book

This is a book about React. But it's not like any other book about React. This is a book about writing React code in a joyful way. You might learn a few new things about React, but that's not my goal. My goal is to help you write better code, and to have more fun doing it.

In Chapter 1, Test-Driven Development with Jest, on page 1, you'll get a taste of test-driven development, a programming methodology that uses tests to create a feedback loop as you work. For our test framework, you'll use the lightning-fast Jest library.

Chapter 2, Integrated Tooling with VS Code, on page 17 will introduce you to some of my favorite tools: VS Code, an amazingly powerful editor; ESLint and Prettier, the ultimate code beautification duo; and Wallaby.js, which I can only describe as pure magic. You'll experience the wonder of instantaneous feedback as you code.

Then in Chapter 3, Testing React with Enzyme, on page 49, you'll start writing React components and testing them with the Enzyme library. You'll get acquainted with Babel, the compiler that lets you write the JavaScript of the future, *today.* You'll build a complex component the TDD way, with 100% code coverage.

Chapter 4, Styling in JavaScript with Styled-Components, on page 89 is all about style. You'll use the styled-components library to add pizzazz to our React components. All of these styles will be defined in JavaScript, making them easy to test. You'll start using one of Jest's most powerful features: snapshots. And you'll set up webpack so that you can view the fruits of your labor in the browser.

In Chapter 5, Refactoring with Higher-Order Components, on page 123, you'll learn some important techniques for refactoring React components. You'll extract pieces of functionality into higher-order components (HOCs), encouraging code reuse and allowing core components to stay small and easy to test. And you'll look at your components with X-ray vision through the power of the React Devtools.

Finally, in Chapter 6, Continuous Integration and Collaboration, on page 147, you'll meet all the tools you'll need to share what you have built with the world. You will run your tests in the cloud with Travis CI, enforce your project's rules with Husky, and create beautiful, interactive documentation with Storybook.

What's Not in This Book

This is not an introduction to JavaScript. If you're new to the language, or if you just want a refresher, I highly recommend Kyle Simpson's excellent *You Don't Know JS*[1] series. Most of the code in this book will employ features added to the language as part of the ECMAScript 6 (also known as ES6 or ES2015) standard. Here's a quick test:

```
const stringifyAll = (...args) => args.map(String);
```

If any of that syntax is confounding, you'll find clarity in the *ES6 & Beyond* volume of Simpson's book series.

Some familiarity with React is helpful, but not required. I'll give a brief explanation for each React concept we encounter. If you want a more thorough introduction, pick up Ludovico Fischer's *React for Real.*[2]

All tests in this book are unit tests, meaning the JavaScript code is tested in isolation. We won't be covering integration tests (e.g., a test where the Java-Script code talks to a database) or functional tests (e.g., a test where a tool like Selenium interacts with the code as it runs in a browser). While I don't quite believe that such tests are a scam,[3] the fact is that they require far more effort to implement, run, and maintain than unit tests. My advice is to achieve a high degree of code coverage with unit tests first, then add more layers of testing as needed.

How to Read the Code Examples

This book takes a hands-on, project-driven approach, which means that source files often change over the course of a chapter. When a code example is a work in progress, its file name (relative to the project root) is shown as a comment at the top of the snippet:

---

1.   https://github.com/getify/You-Dont-Know-JS
2.   https://pragprog.com/book/lfreact/react-for-real
3.   http://blog.thecodewhisperer.com/permalink/integrated-tests-are-a-scam

```
// src/tests/MyComponent.test.js
import React from 'react';
import MyComponent from '../MyComponent';

describe('MyComponent', () => {
  it('renders a <div /> tag', () => {
    const wrapper = shallow(<MyComponent />);
    expect(wrapper.type()).toBe('div');
  });
});
```

As a source file changes over the course of a chapter, familiar sections are omitted with ... and new/edited lines are highlighted:

```
// src/tests/MyComponent.test.js
...

describe('MyComponent', () => {
  ...

  it('accepts a `className` prop', () => {
    const wrapper = shallow(<MyComponent className="test-class" />);
    expect(wrapper.hasClass('test-class')).toBe(true);
  });
});
```

The final version of a source file within a chapter has a download link at the top instead of a comment:

```
intro/src/tests/MyComponent.test.js
import React from 'react';
import MyComponent from '../MyComponent';

describe('MyComponent', () => {
  it('renders a <div /> tag', () => {
    const wrapper = shallow(<MyComponent />);
    expect(wrapper.type()).toBe('div');
  });

  it('accepts a `className` prop', () => {
    const wrapper = shallow(<MyComponent className="test-class" />);
    expect(wrapper.hasClass('test-class')).toBe(true);
  });

  it('triggers `onClick` when clicked', () => {
    const onClick = jest.fn();
    const wrapper = shallow(<MyComponent onClick={onClick} />);
    wrapper.simulate('click');
    expect(onClick).toHaveBeenCalled();
  });
});
```

Online Resources

You can find the source code for the projects in this book on the PragProg website.[4] You can also use the site to report errata. Help make this book better for other readers!

Mantra: Code with Joy

At its best, coding is an exercise in imagination and exploration, an exciting journey into the unknown. At its worst, it feels like stumbling in the dark. Which kind of experience you'll have is largely determined by feedback. The next time you're feeling frustrated, take a step back and ask yourself what kind of feedback would help you move forward. What question can you ask about your code that would bring clarity? Can you turn that question into a test?

I hope this book will help you bring more joy to your work by instilling a habit of seeking feedback early and often. Let's begin!

Trevor Burnham
trevorburnham@gmail.com
Cambridge, MA, June 2019

---

4. https://pragprog.com/book/tbreact/test-driven-react

CHAPTER 1

Test-Driven Development with Jest

Most tests are an afterthought. A programmer writes hundreds of lines of code to add a new feature to an application, followed by a perfunctory test or two. This "test-later" way of working has several drawbacks.

First, without tests, the programmer receives no feedback while writing the feature. If their approach turns out to be a dead-end, they won't know it until they've finished the entire implementation.

Second, the tests the programmer writes after implementing the feature tend to be unthorough and unimaginative. Typically they confirm that the feature works along the "happy path"—that is, when used exactly as anticipated—rather than revealing potential bugs that might occur under edge case conditions.

Lastly, the programmer will be tempted to graft the new feature on to the app rather than rethinking the existing app structure, leading to codebase bloat. Fear of breaking other functionality prevents them from refactoring.

Fortunately, there's an alternative: *Write the tests first!* That's the core tenet of the software development methodology known as test-driven development (TDD). In addition to encouraging thorough test coverage, TDD changes the coding experience by giving you rapid feedback: with your tests already in place, you can quickly find out what works and what doesn't. That gives you the freedom to experiment with different approaches. Experimentation leads to learning, which leads to better code. Plus, it's just more fun!

This book will introduce you to a TDD workflow suited to React development. That means taking full advantage of the extensive range of support tools that have joined the JavaScript ecosystem in the last few years: Jest, ESLint, Prettier, Babel, webpack, and more. Rather than dive into a complete project setup, we'll add these tools one at a time. The goal is for you to understand these tools well enough to feel that you're in control. Ultimately, the tools themselves should fade into the background. What's important is the feedback the tools give you.

In this chapter, you'll build a simple JavaScript project using a test-driven approach. With Jest as your test framework, you'll be able to create a lightning-fast feedback loop. Along the way, you'll learn how to manage dependencies with npm.

Although this chapter's project is extremely simple, the tools introduced here will continue to serve you through the rest of the book. In Chapter 2, Integrated Tooling with VS Code, on page 17, you'll integrate these and other tools into the VS Code editor. All of this preparation will give you a strong foundation when you dive into React development in Chapter 3, Testing React with Enzyme, on page 49.

Introducing Jest

Jest is a test framework developed by Facebook. Thanks to its zippyness and rich feature set, it's quickly become the de facto standard for testing React apps. It's catching on outside of the React ecosystem, too.

Unlike its forerunners (notably Jasmine), which expect to run in a browser environment, Jest runs in a Node.js process. That may seem counterintuitive: Shouldn't code written to be run in the browser be tested in the browser? Short answer: not anymore! It's become possible to simulate browser APIs in Node.js, thanks to a miraculous library called jsdom.[1] The advantages of using a simulated browser environment in Node are huge: tests can be run much more quickly, code coverage can be calculated easily, and the same tests can be run on any system—whether it's a developer's laptop or a continuous integration server—with consistent results.

We'll be using Jest as our test framework throughout this book. In this section, we'll set up a Node project, add Jest as a dependency, and run our first test. No prior experience with Node is required, but you'll need some familiarity with the JavaScript language, including the ES6 arrow function syntax. If you need an introduction, or a refresher, check out Kyle Simpson's *You Don't Know JS*.[2]

Installing Node and npm

The JavaScript landscape has changed dramatically in the last eight years, and nothing bears as much responsibility for all that change as Node.js ("Node"

---

1. https://github.com/jsdom/jsdom
2. https://github.com/getify/You-Dont-Know-JS

for short). JavaScript was created at Netscape in 1995 to run in one specific place: the browser. Since then, server-side JavaScript had been attempted in various forms, but without much success. Node changed all that. Today, JavaScript powers millions of servers, rivals Ruby and Python in popularity as a scripting language, and lies at the core of many rich desktop apps—including VS Code, a full-featured editor you'll meet in the next chapter. Thanks to Node, JavaScript is *everywhere*.

Check if you have Node installed by running node -v:

```
$ node -v
v8.12.0
```

If that command runs and gives you version 8 or higher, you're good to go. If not, go to NodeJS.org[3] to download and install the latest LTS (long-term support) release. If it still doesn't run, you may need to add the node executable to your command-line shell's PATH.[4]

The Node installer should also have included an executable called npm:

```
$ npm -v
6.4.1
```

Officially, npm (never capitalized) is not an acronym. But colloquially, it's known as the *n*ode *p*ackage *m*anager. And as we'll soon see, it's an indispenable tool!

Although we'll be relying on the Node runtime to power many of the tools in this book, we won't be doing much direct interaction with Node's APIs. If you would like to learn to write apps that run on Node, an excellent introduction is Jim R. Wilson's *Node.js 8 the Right Way*.[5]

What about Yarn?

If you're a savvy Node developer, you may have heard of Yarn, another Node package manager that made a big splash when it hit the scene in 2016. Yarn was created to address a number of flaws in npm, notably inconsistency (different users getting different dependency trees for the same project) and slow performance.

Yarn is a terrific project, but open source cross-pollination has narrowed the gap between it and npm. If you're already a die-hard Yarn user, great! Feel free to use the yarn equivalents of the npm commands in this book. But if you don't use Yarn, there's little reason to switch. Just make sure you're on npm version 6 or newer.

---

3. https://nodejs.org/
4. https://cbednarski.com/articles/understanding-environment-variables-and-the-unix-path/
5. https://pragprog.com/book/jwnode2/node-js-8-the-right-way

Creating a Node Project

These days, it's *pro forma* for every JavaScript project—whether intended for the browser, a Node server, or somewhere else—to start the same way: with a package.json. This metadata file contains all of the information about our project that Node might be interested in (such as the "entry point" module that it should run when a script imports our project) as well as several pieces of human-oriented metadata (the description, author, license, etc.). Most importantly for our purposes, npm uses package.json to track dependencies like Jest. Your first project will be called "test-driven-fizzbuzz." Create a directory with that name and cd into it:

```
$ mkdir test-driven-fizzbuzz
$ cd test-driven-fizzbuzz/
```

Create a package.json by running npm init. Press ↵ at each prompt to accept the default response:

```
$ npm init
...
package name: (test-driven-fizzbuzz)
version: (1.0.0)
description:
entry point: (index.js)
test command:
git repository:
keywords:
author:
license: (ISC)
...
Is this OK? (yes)
```

There's one tweak you'll want to make to the generated package.json. Assuming you don't plan on publishing this project to the npm registry, add the line "private": true (followed by a comma to avoid breaking the JSON syntax):

```
// package.json
{
  "name": "test-driven-fizzbuzz",
➤ "private": true,
  "version": "1.0.0",
  "description": "",
  "main": "index.js",
  "scripts": {
    "test": "echo \"Error: no test specified\" && exit 1"
  },
  "author": "",
  "license": "ISC"
}
```

The private flag prevents accidental publication and silences several npm warnings about our package not being publication-ready. It's a good practice to declare all new Node projects as private, then remove the private flag if and when you decide to publish.

Adding Jest as a Dependency

Use npm to install the jest package:

```
❶ $ npm install --save-dev jest@23.6.0
  ...
❷ npm created a lockfile as package-lock.json. You should commit this file.

  + jest@23.6.0
❸ added 538 packages from 269 contributors in 24.446s
```

❶ The --save-dev flag tells npm, "I want to use the jest package for development only. My project doesn't need it at runtime." The jest@23.6.0 means "I want version 23.6.0 of the jest package."

❷ For reasons that are too involved to go into here, the information in package.json isn't enough for two machines to be guaranteed to get the same node_modules, even if you specify exact versions for all dependencies. That's why npm creates the lockfile. If you're curious about the details, check out the npm docs.[6]

❸ The "538 packages" figure is striking, but it's *de rigeur* for Node packages: You depend on one package, which depends on several other packages, which each in turn depend on several more, and so on. npm recursively installs all of them! If you're curious to see what all these packages are, take a peek at the freshly created node_modules directory.

If you open up package.json again, you'll see that npm has created a new entry called devDependencies:

```
// package.json
{
  ...
  "devDependencies": {
❶   "jest": "^23.6.0"
  }
}
```

❶ By default, npm lists dependencies in package.json with a caret (^) version range.[7] In this case, that means that any release of jest from version 23.6.0

---

6. https://docs.npmjs.com/files/package-locks
7. https://docs.npmjs.com/misc/semver#caret-ranges-123-025-004

up to but not including 24.0.0 will satisfy the dependency. In principle, this shouldn't cause any problems because projects should bump their major version when making any breaking change. In practice, projects often don't.

If you'd prefer that npm omit the caret and use exact version specifiers, you can modify your npm config with this command:

```
$ npm config set save-exact true
```

If you were to delete node_modules, you could easily recover its contents by running npm install, which installs every package listed as a dependency in package.json.

Now Jest is installed and ready for you to use. However, it's in the project's node_modules, not on your PATH. To run it, you'll need to call on another tool: npx.

Running Package Binaries with npx

In 2017, the npm team introduced a sibling project: npx.[8] Whereas npm is a package manager, npx is a package *runner*. Among other things, npx lets you run binaries from local Node packages without adding them to your PATH.

Try running Jest with the npx command:

```
$ npx jest
No tests found
In /Users/tburnham/code/test-driven-fizzbuzz
  7 files checked.
  testMatch: **/__tests__/**/*.js?(x),**/?(*.)+(spec|test).js?(x) - 0 matches
  testPathIgnorePatterns: /node_modules/ - 7 matches
Pattern:  - 0 matches
```

Any extra arguments you provide are passed to the executable that's being run with npx:

```
$ npx jest --version
23.5.0
```

If you've been doing JavaScript development without npx, you'll find that it's an essential addition to your toolbelt.

Running Project Scripts with npm

While npx provides a convenient solution for running local binaries, it's also useful to document the most common commands that use those binaries.

---

8.   https://blog.npmjs.org/post/162869356040/introducing-npx-an-npm-package-runner

The best way to do that is to list those commands in the scripts section of your project's package.json.

Scripts listed in scripts can be executed with npm run <script>. That spawns a shell process that has all of the executables from node_modules in its PATH, making npx unnecessary.

Go ahead and replace the placeholder "test" script that npm init generated with jest, producing the final package.json for the chapter:

```
ch1/package.json
{
  "name": "test-driven-fizzbuzz",
  "private": true,
  "version": "1.0.0",
  "description": "",
  "main": "index.js",
  "scripts": {
    "test": "jest"
  },
  "author": "",
  "license": "ISC",
  "devDependencies": {
    "jest": "^23.6.0"
  },
  "dependencies": {}
}
```

The test script is special to npm: You can execute it with either npm run test or just npm test. Try it now:

```
$ npm test

> test-driven-fizzbuzz@1.0.0 test /Users/tburnham/code/test-driven-fizzbuzz
> jest

No tests found
In /Users/tburnham/code/test-driven-fizzbuzz
  7 files checked.
  testMatch: **/__tests__/**/*.js?(x),**/?(*.)+(spec|test).js?(x) - 0 matches
  testPathIgnorePatterns: /node_modules/ - 7 matches
Pattern:  - 0 matches
npm ERR! Test failed.  See above for more details.
```

❶ When you run a script with npm, all npm cares about is the exit code. In this case, because no tests were found, Jest returned a non-zero exit code, which npm interprets as failure.

In Chapter 6, Continuous Integration and Collaboration, on page 147, you'll learn how to run your project scripts in the cloud.

Writing a Test

Time for your first test! Create a file called greeting.test.js:

```
// greeting.test.js
const greeting = guest => `Hello, ${guest}!`;

describe('greeting()', () => {
  it('says hello', () => {
    expect(greeting('Jest')).toBe('Hello, Jest!');
  });
});
```

❶ describe() declares a *test suite*, which is a grouping of tests. Its first argument is a name, and the second is a function containing one or more tests.

❷ it() declares a *test*. Its first argument is a name, and the second is a function with the actual test code.

❸ expect() creates an *assertion*. It takes a single argument, typically a value generated by the code being tested, and returns an object that exposes a set of matcher functions.

toBe() is a *matcher* that performs a strict equality test between the value being tested (the expect() argument) and the expected value (its own argument).

Note the grammatical convention here: the test suite name ("greeting()") is a noun; the test name ("says hello") is a verb. Together, they form a complete sentence describing the functionality covered by the test ("greeting() says hello"). This convention helps make test output easy to read. You can learn more about all of these methods in the Jest API docs.[9]

To run the test, all you need to do is invoke the jest CLI. By default, it finds and runs every file in the current project with the .test.js extension. Since you set jest as the test script in package.json, you can run it with npm run test:

```
$ npm test
...
 PASS  ./greeting.test.js
  greeting()
    ✓ says hello (3ms)

Test Suites: 1 passed, 1 total
Tests:       1 passed, 1 total
Snapshots:   0 total
Time:        0.83s
Ran all test suites.
```

---

9. https://jestjs.io/docs/en/api

Excellent! Jest found the test file, ran the test, and confirmed that greeting('Jest') produces the string 'Hello, Jest!'.

You can go ahead and delete greeting.test.js. In the next section, we'll start building this chapter's project.

The Tao of Test-Driven Development

Test-driven development (TDD) is sometimes defined as writing tests first. Although that's an important part of the methodology, it's not the essence. The essence of TDD is rapid iteration. You'll find that you learn more quickly from iterating—writing small, easy-to-understand pieces of code one at a time—than you would from trying to plan out a complex program from the ground up. You'll discover bad assumptions and potential pitfalls before you invest too much work. And you'll find the process more enjoyable, a smooth incremental progression rather than an alternation between bursts of inspiration and plateaus of "What do I do next?"

Our project for this chapter will be a solver for the classic programming challenge Fizz Buzz.[10] Here are the rules of Fizz Buzz:

> Write a program that prints the numbers from 1 to 100. But for multiples of three print "Fizz" instead of the number and for the multiples of five print "Buzz." For numbers which are multiples of both three and five print "FizzBuzz."

If that sounds simple to you, congratulations: you're a programmer!

In this section, you'll apply the TDD process to implementing a function that takes a number and returns the appropriate Fizz Buzz output. First, you'll write a single test, knowing that it'll fail. Second, you'll write an implementation that satisfies the test. Once the test is passing, you'll use Git to save your progress.

Starting from Failure

Create an index.js with a placeholder implementation of fizzBuzz(), so that your tests will have a valid referent:

```
// index.js
module.exports = (num) => `${num}`;
```

Now add an index.test.js with a test for a single Fizz Buzz rule:

---

10. http://wiki.c2.com/?FizzBuzzTest

```
// index.test.js
const fizzBuzz = require('./index');

describe('fizzBuzz()', () => {
  it('returns "FizzBuzz" for multiples of 3 and 5', () => {
    expect(fizzBuzz(15)).toBe('FizzBuzz');
    expect(fizzBuzz(30)).toBe('FizzBuzz');
  });
});
```

Run the test:

```
$ npm test
...
 FAIL  ./index.test.js
  fizzBuzz()
    ✕ returns "FizzBuzz" for multiples of 3 and 5 (7ms)

  ● fizzBuzz() › returns "FizzBuzz" for multiples of 3 and 5

    expect(received).toBe(expected) // Object.is equality

    Expected value to be:
      "FizzBuzz"
    Received:
      "15"

      3 | describe('fizzBuzz()', () => {
      4 |   it('returns "FizzBuzz" for multiples of 3 and 5', () => {
    > 5 |     expect(fizzBuzz(15)).toBe('FizzBuzz');
      6 |     expect(fizzBuzz(30)).toBe('FizzBuzz');
      7 |   });
      8 | });

      at Object.it (index.test.js:5:32)

Test Suites: 1 failed, 1 total
Tests:       1 failed, 1 total
Snapshots:   0 total
Time:        0.771s, estimated 1s
Ran all test suites.
```

You may have cringed when you saw that glowing red FAIL. After all, having tests fail against production code is bad. But having tests fail during development can be a good thing! It means that you've anticipated some way your code *could* fail. Think of every failing test you see during development as a potential bug you've preemptively squashed.

Running Jest Tests Automatically

Jumping to the console every time you want to run some tests is a chore. Happily, Jest has a "watch mode" in which it automatically re-runs all tests when it detects any change to a test file, or to a source file depended on by a test.

To start Jest in watch mode, run it with the --watchAll flag:

```
$ npx jest --watchAll
```

Now you should see the same failure result as before. Try saving either index.js or index.test.js, and the test will re-run. (Blink and you might miss it!) You can press q at any time to quit. For now, leave Jest watch mode running.

Getting to Green

Since Jest is watching your project, see if you can tackle the "'FizzBuzz'" test case:

```
// index.js
➤ module.exports = (num) => {
➤   if (num % 15 === 0) return 'FizzBuzz';
➤   return `${num}`
➤ };
```

As soon as you hit save, your console output should change:

```
 PASS  ./index.test.js
  fizzBuzz()
    ✓ returns "FizzBuzz" for multiples of 3 and 5

Test Suites: 1 passed, 1 total
Tests:       1 passed, 1 total
Snapshots:   0 total
Time:        0.121s, estimated 1s
Ran all test suites.
```

Achievement unlocked: you've just completed a test-driven development cycle!

Measuring Test Coverage

A great feature of Jest is its built-in code coverage measurement. This shows you how much of the code being tested actually ran during tests. To compute code coverage, add the --coverage flag. By default, this saves a report to a coverage directory, as well as showing a summary in the console. To just get that summary output, use the flag --coverageReporters=text:

```
$ npm run test -- --coverage --coverageReporters=text
 PASS  ./index.test.js
  fizzBuzz()
    ✓ returns "FizzBuzz" for multiples of 3 and 5
```

File	% Stmts	% Branch	% Funcs	% Lines	Uncovered Line #s
All files	75	50	100	66.67	
index.js	75	50	100	66.67	3

```
Test Suites: 1 passed, 1 total
Tests:       1 passed, 1 total
Snapshots:   0 total
Time:        0.121s, estimated 1s
Ran all test suites.
```

Here the report shows 75% of statements were covered, and 50% of branches. "Branches" refer to the possible outcomes of if/else statements. The 50% result reflects the fact that the current test only covers the case where the condition num % 15 === 0 passes. Try adding a test to cover the case where it fails:

```
// index.test.js
const fizzBuzz = require('../index');

describe('fizzBuzz()', () => {
  it('returns "FizzBuzz" for multiples of 3 and 5', () => {
    expect(fizzBuzz(15)).toBe('FizzBuzz');
    expect(fizzBuzz(30)).toBe('FizzBuzz');
  });

➤  it('returns the given number for multiples of neither 3 nor 5', () => {
➤    expect(fizzBuzz(1)).toBe('1');
➤    expect(fizzBuzz(22)).toBe('22');
➤  });
});
```

Then run the test with code coverage again:

```
$ npm run test -- --coverage --coverageReporters=text
 PASS  tests/index.test.js
  fizzBuzz()
    ✓ returns "FizzBuzz" for multiples of 3 and 5 (3ms)
    ✓ returns the given number for multiples of neither 3 nor 5 (1ms)
```

File	% Stmts	% Branch	% Funcs	% Lines	Uncovered Line #s
All files	100	100	100	100	
index.js	100	100	100	100	

```
Test Suites: 1 passed, 1 total
Tests:       2 passed, 2 total
Snapshots:   0 total
Time:        1.01s
Ran all test suites.
```

Perfect! The report confirms that every possible code path was taken when the tests ran.

Like all metrics, code coverage is imperfect—projects with impressive code coverage numbers don't necessarily have the most *useful* tests—but the numbers can still guide you in the right direction. It's especially handy for identifying parts of your project with large gaps in test coverage.

Checking in Changes

Whenever you add a new test and get it to pass, that's a good time to get your project into source control. That way, no matter what you do to the project, you can always restore it to the all-green state later.

We'll use Git as our source control system in this book. If you're not familiar with Git, you might want to read through the "Git Basics" section of the excellent *Pro Git* by Scott Chacon and Ben Straub.[11]

The first step is initializing this project as a Git repository:

```
$ git init
Initialized empty Git repository in
/Users/tburnham/code/test-driven-fizzbuzz/.git/
```

Don't commit just yet. If you run git status, you'll notice that there are a *staggering* number of files! Remember those "538 packages" npm mentioned when you installed Jest? They're all hanging out in the project's node_modules directory. Fortunately, we don't need to keep those in source control, because all of the information needed to re-create the node_modules tree is contained in package-lock.json. So tell Git to ignore the installed packages by creating a .gitignore file at the root of the project:

ch1/.gitignore
```
node_modules/
```

There. Now the project looks a lot more manageable, from Git's point of view:

```
$ git status
On branch master

No commits yet

Untracked files:
  (use "git add <file>..." to include in what will be committed)

        .gitignore
        index.js
        index.test.js
        package-lock.json
        package.json

nothing added to commit but untracked files present (use "git add" to track)
```

---

11. https://git-scm.com/book/en/v1/Getting-Started-Git-Basics

All of those files belong in source control, so stage them for commit:

```
$ git add .
```

Just for fun, this book uses the recommended gitmoji[12] for all of its commit messages. These are ASCII-friendly aliases that render as emoji on GitHub and in some other tools. For a project's first commit, the appropriate gitmoji is :tada:, which represents the "Party Popper" emoji:[13]

```
$ git commit -m ":tada: First commit"
[master (root-commit) dca2255] :tada: First commit
 5 files changed, 5893 insertions(+)
 create mode 100644 .gitignore
 create mode 100644 index.js
 create mode 100644 index.test.js
 create mode 100644 package-lock.json
 create mode 100644 package.json
```

Congrats on completing your first feature! You wrote a test for the feature, made the test pass, and then checked that change into source control. Satisfying, isn't it?

As an exercise, see if you can repeat the TDD process for the remaining Fizz Buzz requirements. Namely, your fizzBuzz() function should return:

1. "Fizz" for multiples of 3,
2. "Buzz" for multiples of 5, and
3. The given number for multiples of neither 3 nor 5

For each of those requirements, add a test within the same suite (the describe() block), modify the implementation to make everything pass, then move to the next requirement. You can find an example solution at the end of the chapter.

Mantra: Red, Green, Repeat

Each chapter of this book concludes with a mantra, a phrase you can repeat to yourself whenever you're feeling unfocused to bring clarity. This chapter's mantra—*"Red, green, repeat"*—encapsulates test-driven development (TDD) in a nutshell. Whenever you feel stuck, let the mantra guide you. In the long term, the habit of putting tests first helps to form a healthy mindset for problem solving, one in which failing code evokes curiosity instead of despair.

In the abstract, the act of writing tests before code may seem inconsequential. Writing code and writing tests are, one might imagine, two activities that can

---

12. https://gitmoji.carloscuesta.me/
13. https://emojipedia.org/party-popper/

be done in any order with identical results. But imagining is one thing; hands-on experience is another. If you've done the exercise for this chapter, and taken advantage of Jest's watch mode, then you know the feeling of satisfaction at watching a test flip from red to green as your code clicks into place.

And it doesn't have to stop there. With the new code still fresh in your mind, you can experiment. Try a different approach. Use cleaner syntax. Refactor. As soon as you save, the test console will tell you if your revision is viable. With just a few extra minutes, you can almost always find a way to make your code better. More importantly, what you learn from these little ventures will make you a better coder.

The entire TDD methodology is made possible by rapid feedback. But tests aren't the only possible source of that feedback. In the next chapter, you'll get to know ESLint, an automated checker for good coding practices. And you'll find out how you can integrate feedback from both ESLint and Jest directly into your code editor.

Example Fizz Buzz Solution

ch1/index.test.js
```
const fizzBuzz = require('./index');

describe('fizzBuzz()', () => {
  it('returns "FizzBuzz" for multiples of 3 and 5', () => {
    expect(fizzBuzz(15)).toBe('FizzBuzz');
    expect(fizzBuzz(30)).toBe('FizzBuzz');
  });

  it('returns "Fizz" for multiples of 3', () => {
    expect(fizzBuzz(3)).toBe('Fizz');
    expect(fizzBuzz(33)).toBe('Fizz');
  });

  it('returns "Buzz" for multiples of 5', () => {
    expect(fizzBuzz(5)).toBe('Buzz');
    expect(fizzBuzz(20)).toBe('Buzz');
  });

  it('returns the given number for multiples of neither 3 nor 5', () => {
    expect(fizzBuzz(1)).toBe('1');
    expect(fizzBuzz(22)).toBe('22');
  });
});
```

ch1/index.js
```
module.exports = (num) => {
  if (num % 15 === 0) return 'FizzBuzz';
  if (num % 3 === 0) return 'Fizz';
  if (num % 5 === 0) return 'Buzz';
  return `${num}`
};
```

CHAPTER 2

Integrated Tooling with VS Code

As we learned in the previous chapter, the essence of test-driven development is rapid iteration. Instead of waiting until you've churned out a whole feature before finding out if your code works, you split that feature into small pieces and enjoy feedback as you put each piece in place.

Ideally, the kind of feedback used for TDD should be automated (no effort required) and fast (no waiting). We've seen how helpful Jest's watch mode is in both regards. But you can do even better, by incorporating feedback directly into your code editing environment.

This chapter is about that environment. It starts with VS Code, a powerful and highly customizable editor. Later in the chapter, you'll incorporate some new tools into this coding environment: ESLint (which detects common coding mistakes) and Prettier (which auto-formats code so you can stay focused on substance over style). Last but not least, you'll experience Wallaby, a magical piece of software that bridges the gap between your code and your tests to give you real-time feedback.

The goal is to get you acquainted with all of the pieces of a modern JavaScript development stack. Although this chapter is a bit of a detour, you'll find the arsenal of support tools introduced here invaluable when you take on the challenge of React development, starting in Chapter 3, Testing React with Enzyme, on page 49.

If you're already comfortable with your development environment, feel free to skim this chapter. The aim here isn't to convince you to switch to VS Code but rather to minimize the friction between you and your tools, by setting up your testing library and linter to silently watch over your code. If you need to run a command to see your test results, you can do better.

Editing with VS Code

Microsoft's Visual Studio Code (VS Code for short) is a relatively new entry in the world of code editors. First launched in 2015, it rapidly rose to become one of the most popular editors in the JavaScript community—in fact the *most* popular, according to the State of JavaScript 2018 survey.[1] What makes VS Code special is its incredible extensibility. There's a rich ecosystem of VS Code extensions, especially for JavaScript development, as we'll soon see.

> ### Visual Studio vs. VS Code
>
> Don't confuse Visual Studio Code with Visual Studio. The two are about as similar as JavaScript and Java, another oddly co-branded pair. Whereas Visual Studio is an enterprise-grade commercial IDE made for Windows, VS Code is a sleek, cross-platform text editor inspired by Sublime Text and Atom. It's also completely open source.[a]
>
> ———————
>
> a.   https://github.com/microsoft/vscode

In this section, we'll get to know VS Code as we use it to start a new test-driven JavaScript project.

Launching VS Code and the Integrated Terminal

To get started, download and install the latest VS Code release.[2] Open it up and take a look around. We'll only cover the essentials of the editor in this book; for more details on everything you're looking at, see the User Interface[3] page in the official docs.

The most important feature to know about in VS Code is the *Command Palette*, as seen in the screenshot on page 19. The Command Palette is a single searchable list of every command that VS Code supports. Any time you hear a command referenced by name, you can find and execute it from the Command Palette. To open the Command Palette, type ⇧⌘P (macOS) or ⇧^P (Windows and Linux). Alternatively, you can click the gear icon in the lower-left corner of the workspace and select "Command Palette..." from the context menu.

If another editor's built-in keyboard shortcuts are ingrained in your muscle memory, you can make the transition to VS Code easier by installing a keymap.

———————

1.   https://2018.stateofjs.com/other-tools/#text_editors
2.   https://code.visualstudio.com
3.   https://code.visualstudio.com/docs/getstarted/userinterface

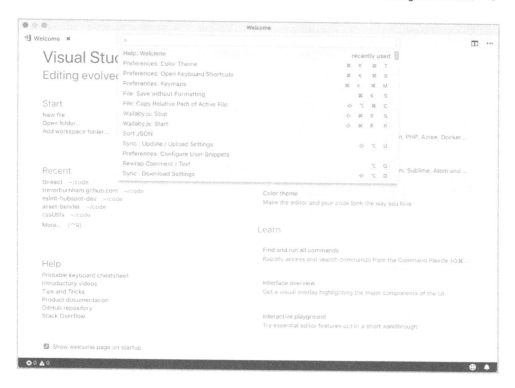

Keymaps are a type of VS Code extension that add key bindings. From the Command Palette, select "Preferences: Keymaps." A list of all available keymaps will appear in the sidebar. Click the green Install button for the one corresponding to your favorite (for now) editor, then click the blue Restart button that replaces it. Now those familiar keyboard shortcuts are at your ready.

If you're on macOS, there's one other VS Code command you should run right away: "Shell Command: Install code command in PATH." The code utility lets you open files and directories in VS Code from the command line. If you're on Windows or Linux, code should have already been installed for you.

Now take another look around. Most of the workspace is occupied by the editor area. By default, that area is occupied by a Welcome page. Close that tab. With no files open, the editor area shows a handy list of commonly used keyboard shortcuts, as seen in the screenshot on page 20.

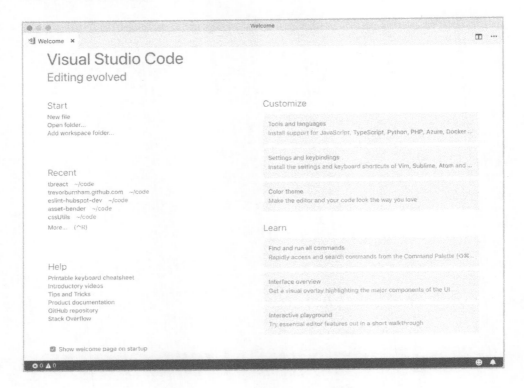

Try one of those now, "Toggle Terminal" (^`). A shell will pop up from the bottom of the screen. For any developer used to switching back and forth between their editor and their terminal, this integrated terminal is a game-changer. Try using it to create the directory for this chapter's project, test-driven-palindromes:

```
$ mkdir test-driven-palindromes
```

Then open that directory using the code command-line utility. By default, code [dir] opens dir in a new window; since we don't need our existing workspace, add the -r flag (short for --reuse-window):

```
$ code -r test-driven-palindromes
```

Now VS Code knows that you're working on a project in the test-driven-palindromes directory, which lets the editor help you out in a number of ways. For a start, every Terminal instance now opens with test-driven-palindromes as its working directory. Try it:

```
$ pwd
/Users/tburnham/code/test-driven-palindromes
```

Let's start building our new project. The first file we'll need is a package.json.
Use npm init -y to create one with all of the defaults:

```
$ npm init -y
Wrote to /Users/tburnham/code/test-driven-palindromes/package.json:

{
  "name": "test-driven-palindromes",
  "version": "1.0.0",
  "description": "",
  "main": "index.js",
  "scripts": {
    "test": "echo \"Error: no test specified\" && exit 1"
  },
  "keywords": [],
  "author": "",
  "license": "ISC"
}
```

Open the new package.json by clicking it in the Explorer sidebar, or you can
use the handy "Go to File" command (⌘P on macOS, ^P on Windows and
Linux) to search for it. As in Chapter 1, add a "private": true entry, keeping in
mind that JSON requires a comma at the end of every entry. (If you forget,
VS Code will helpfully highlight the invalid JSON syntax in red to remind
you.) Then install Jest:

```
$ npm install --save-dev jest@23.6.0
```

Finally, replace the boilerplate "test" script with "jest", as in the previous
chapter:

```
// package.json
{
  "name": "test-driven-palindromes",
➤ "private": true,
  "version": "1.0.0",
  "description": "",
  "main": "index.js",
  "scripts": {
➤   "test": "jest"
  },
  "keywords": [],
  "author": "",
  "license": "ISC",
  "devDependencies": {
    "jest": "^23.6.0"
  }
}
```

Then toggle the terminal again (^`) to get it out of the way. You won't need it for the next section.

Using Editor Groups

Let's get back into the rhythm of TDD. For our project, we're going to write a function that finds all palindromes in a string. A palindrome is a phrase that's spelled the same forwards and backwards (ignoring spaces and punctuation). For example:

```
palindromes('What number is never odd or even, asked the Sphinx?')
```

would return

```
['neveroddoreven']
```

As frivolous as a program for finding palindromes may sound, it's a good approximation of a real project in one important sense: the requirements aren't precisely defined. Whereas Fizz Buzz had crystal-clear rules that we could translate directly into tests, figuring out a reasonable set of rules for the palindrome finder will require creativity and experimentation.

Create a "New Untitled File" (⌘N on macOS, ^N on Windows and Linux), then save it (⌘S on macOS, ^S on Windows and Linux) as palindromes.js. Repeat for palindromes.test.js.

Now let's try viewing the two files side-by-side: palindromes.js on the left, palindromes.test.js on the right. There are several ways to do this. If you're a mouse person, the fastest way is to click-and-drag the palindromes.test.js tab to the right edge of the editor area. If you'd rather stick with the keyboard, trigger the "Move Editor into Right Group" command from the Command Palette.

Now all the relevant parts of the project are in view. You can move the focus to different editor groups by pressing the primary modifier key (⌘ on macOS, ^ on Windows and Linux) with the number corresponding to the group's ordinal position. So palindromes.js is ⌘1 or ^1, and palindromes.test.js is ⌘2 or ^2. This even works from the Terminal.

In palindromes.test.js, create the first test:

```
// palindromes.test.js
const palindromes = require('./palindromes')

describe('palindromes()', () => {
  it('correctly identifies one-word palindromes', () => {
    expect(palindromes('madam')).toEqual(['madam']);
  });
});
```

❶ Previously, we've made equality assertions with toBe(). However, toBe() does a strict equality check, which would fail here. The toEqual() assertion method, by contrast, checks for deep object equality. So the assertion expect(x).toEqual(['madam']) passes as long as x is an array with the string "madam" as its only entry.

In palindromes.js, write a placeholder implementation:

```
// palindromes.js
module.exports = (str) => {
  return [str];
};
```

Then open the integrated Terminal and start Jest in watch mode:

```
$ npx jest --watchAll
```

The resulting layout should resemble the following screenshot, with your code and test output visible all at once:

The test should light up green. Time to check your work in! In the next section, we'll see how VS Code streamlines common Git tasks.

Integrated Source Control

VS Code features superb Git integration right out of the box. Stage changes, make commits, view diffs, switch branches, push to remotes—you can do it all without even opening the Terminal. Try opening the Command Palette and typing "git" to get a sense of all the power at your disposal.

Before you initialize Git for your new project, you'll need to do some preemptive ignoring. That node_modules directory is going to gum up the works if you let it. So create a .gitignore file, just like the one in the previous chapter's project:

```
# .gitignore
node_modules/
```

Now use the Command Palette to run "Git: Initialize Repository." When you're prompted to choose a directory, accept the default. This is equivalent to running git init from the command line in the project directory.

With Git initialized, the branch icon on the left edge of the window comes to life, showing a badge with the number 5. This is the number of files with uncommitted changes (which, since we have no commits yet, is all non-ignored files). Click that icon or press ^⇧G to open the Source Control sidebar, as seen in the following screenshot:

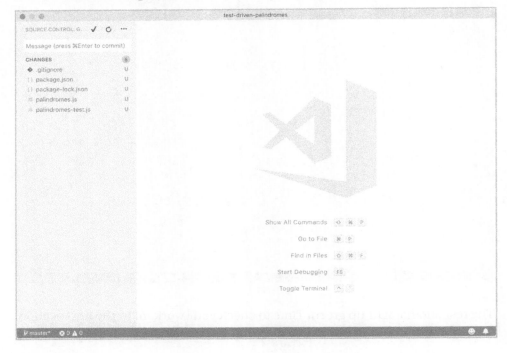

The Source Control sidebar shows you a list of modified files. You can click any of the file names to see a diff view, showing exactly what changes you can stage for commit. You could hover each of the files and click the + icon to stage it, but since you want to stage and commit everything, there is a faster way. Type this commit message into the "Message" box above the list of changes:

```
:tada: First commit
```

Confirm the commit by pressing ⌘↵ (macOS) or ^↵ (Windows and Linux). You'll get a prompt asking if you'd like for VS Code to automatically stage all your changes before committing. Select "Always." This will write an entry in your User Settings, which is the subject of the next subsection.

User Settings

A code editor is only as good as a developer's ability to tailor it to their needs. The VS Code team, knowing this, designed for customizability. All user-level customizations live in a single, editable JSON file, with the exception of keyboard shortcuts, which have their own dedicated customization file.

Recent versions of VS Code added a friendly, graphical settings interface. However, it's useful to see what lurks underneath. From the Command Palette, run "Preferences: Open Settings (JSON)." This opens up a JSON file with all of your personal setting overrides. Since this view doesn't show you the default setting, though, it's not very useful by itself. You can remedy that by adding this setting:

```
"workbench.settings.useSplitJSON": true
```

Save the file and reopen the settings file. Now you'll be taken to a split view, with VS Code's default settings on the left and your user-level overrides on the right, as shown in the first screenshot on page 26.

If you chose "Always" at the Git commit prompt in the last section, then there will be one other override here: git.enableSmartCommit is set to true. Hovering over the rule's name gives you a description of its meaning:

```
Commit all changes when there are no staged changes.
```

If you'd like to change the look and feel of the editor, now's your chance! Let's say you want to change the font. Type "font" in the search bar, and you'll see several matching settings. Hover over any of the matches and click the pencil icon to copy that setting over to your User Settings, where you can do with it what you like. For example, if 12px is a bit squint-inducing for you, you might copy editor.fontSize to your User Settings and change the value to 14. As soon as you save, the change will take effect, as shown in the second screenshot on page 26.

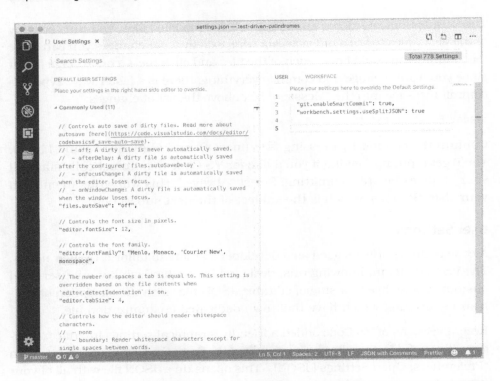

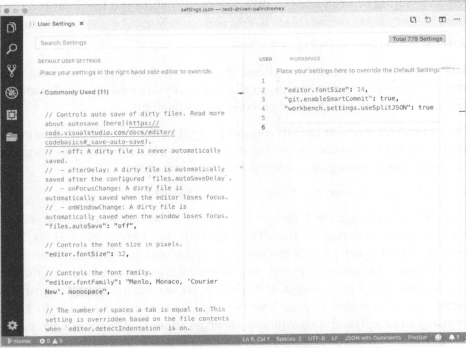

You can also change the color theme (used for both UI and syntax highlighting) via the workbench.colorTheme setting. However, there's a useful shortcut: use the "Color Theme" command, accessible from the context menu on the gear in the lower-left corner. You'll be presented with a list of every installed theme. You can preview them by using ↑ and ↓ to highlight each one, as in the following screenshot:

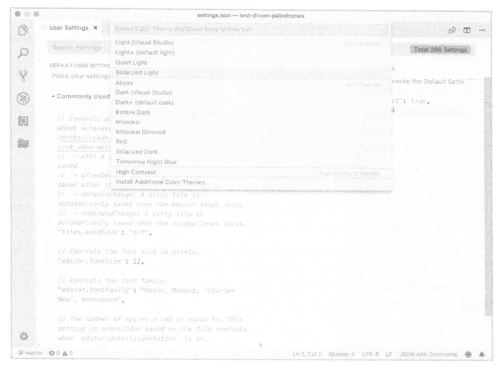

If none of the themes included with VS Code suit you, you can find many more in the VS Code marketplace.[4]

Aside from typography and color choice, perhaps nothing provokes as much developer passion as shells, at least among us Mac devotees. If you want to make the integrated Terminal launch something other than the version of Bash that came with the OS, override the terminal.integrated.shell.osx setting to point to your favorite shell.

One more setting of note: you've probably noticed the smiley face in the lower-right corner, soliciting feedback for the VS Code team. Many developers find it annoying. If you're one of them, just right-click it and select "Hide" from

---

4. https://marketplace.visualstudio.com/search?target=VSCode

the context menu. This'll add an override for the workbench.statusBar.feedback.visible setting:

```
// User Settings
{
    "git.enableSmartCommit": true,
    "workbench.settings.useSplitJSON": true,
    "workbench.statusBar.feedback.visible": false,
}
```

Once you have VS Code adjusted to your liking, we'll make some project-level tweaks.

Workspace Settings

Sometimes you'll want to change an editor setting for a particular project. In VS Code, this feature is called Workspace Settings. Entries in Workspace Settings take precedence over User Settings.

Next to the User Settings heading above the right editor pane, you'll notice that there's a Workspace Settings heading. Click it. As soon as you do, a new file will materialize in the project: .vscode/settings.json. You add overrides to this file the same way that you do with User Settings.

One good use of Workspace Settings is telling VS Code to ignore non-editable files that live in the project via the files.exclude setting. For our purposes, the node_modules directory and package-lock.json are both non-editable, since we want npm to manage them for us:

```
// .vscode/settings.json
{
    "files.exclude": {
        "node_modules": true,
        "package-lock.json": true
    }
}
```

❶ Object settings like this one don't replace the default; instead, the two objects are merged. To remove a key from the default files.exclude. object, copy its key and set the value to false.

Open the Explorer sidebar. You'll notice that node_modules and package-lock.json are gone. They'll also be excluded from all searches, including "Go to File" (though node_modules was already excluded from searches, thanks to the default search.exclude setting). It's worth emphasizing that files.exclude and .gitignore are completely independent: Git will continue to monitor package-lock.json, which means that changes to that file will continue to be listed in the Source Control sidebar.

Another good use of Workspace Settings is indentation. VS Code defaults to using four-space indentation when it can't automatically detect the existing indentation level of a file. Since this book uses two-space indentation for all JavaScript code, try adding a Workspace Setting that stipulates two-space indentation only within JavaScript files:

```
// .vscode/settings.json
{
    "files.exclude": {
        "node_modules": true,
        "package-lock.json": true
    },
    "[javascript]": {
        "editor.tabSize": 2
    }
}
```

❶ The [javascript] key tells VS Code, "Apply all settings within this block only to JavaScript files."

In general, the Workspace Settings file shouldn't be checked into source control, since individual contributors to the same project may want different project-level customizations. So open .gitignore and add the .vscode directory:

ch2/.gitignore
```
node_modules/
.vscode/
```

Now switch to the Source Control sidebar and commit, using the appropriate gitmoji for .gitignore changes:

```
:see_no_evil: Ignore .vscode dir
```

This concludes our whirlwind tour of VS Code's most essential features. You've learned how to use the super-convenient integrated terminal and source control, how to jump to files without touching the mouse, and how to open editors in a side-by-side split view. Most importantly, you realized the power to adjust every little detail of the editor to your liking through User Settings and Workspace Settings.

In the rest of the chapter, you'll go beyond the out-of-the-box capabilities of VS Code by adding extensions specifically tailored for a refined JavaScripting experience.

Checking Code Quality with ESLint

A linter is a program that uses a set of rules to detect code that, though syntactically valid, is likely to contain mistakes. A classic example is using = (assignment) instead of == or === (equality) in an if statement:

```
if (savings = 0) {
  // This "condition" would empty your account!
}
```

Linting JavaScript is especially valuable because of its relatively freewheeling nature. If you mistype window as wimdow, your program won't refuse to run; it just won't run the way you'd hoped. Of course, one way to avoid such fat-finger bugs is to have extensive test coverage. But a linter can often identify such problems sooner, and give you more helpful information for fixing them. Enter ESLint.[5]

Although other JavaScript linters have been tried before, ESLint is the first to really take off, thanks to its pluggable architecture. There are plugins for React, Angular, and every other popular JavaScript framework, aimed at warning developers against the most common gotchas. And what do you know? There's a Jest plugin, too!

You'll find that linting is an invaluable addition to your TDD toolbelt—one that you'll continue to use throughout this book. In this section, you'll learn how to run ESLint, how to configure it, and how to integrate it with VS Code for fast, automatic feedback.

Installing and Configuring ESLint

Let's add ESLint to our project. First, open the VS Code Terminal. If Jest is running in watch mode, press Q to quit. Then install the eslint package:

```
$ npm install --save-dev eslint@5.10.0
+ eslint@5.10.0
```

You can try running ESLint with npx eslint ., but it won't do anything yet—the project needs an ESLint configuration first. Create a new file and save it as .eslintrc.js:

```
// .eslintrc.js
module.exports = {
  extends: ['eslint:recommended'],
};
```

---

5.   https://eslint.org/

This tells ESLint to use its recommended rule set as the base for our config-uration. For a complete list of the included rules, check the ESLint docs.[6] We'll tweak those rules in the next section. Try linting palindromes.js now using the npm lint script:

```
$ npx eslint palindromes.js
/Users/tburnham/code/test-driven-palindromes/palindromes.js
  1:25  error  Parsing error: Unexpected token >

✘ 1 problem (1 error, 0 warnings)
```

ESLint refused to parse the arrow function syntax, (expression) => { ... }. By default, ESLint makes the conservative assumption that all code must conform to the ECMAScript 5 standard; arrow functions were added in ECMAScript 6. To change that assumption, add a new entry called parseOptions to the ESLint configuration:

```
// .eslintrc.js
module.exports = {
  extends: ['eslint:recommended'],
  parserOptions: {
    ecmaVersion: 6,
  },
};
```

Run the linter again, and you'll see a different error:

```
$ npx eslint palindromes.js
/Users/tburnham/code/test-driven-palindromes/palindromes.js
  1:1  error  'module' is not defined  no-undef

✘ 1 problem (1 error, 0 warnings)
```

Once again, ESLint is erring on the side of caution. The module global isn't part of any ECMAScript standard, and would indeed be undefined in many environ-ments. We expect it to be defined, however, because this code will run in a Node environment. To let ESLint know that, add an entry called env to its configuration:

```
// .eslintrc.js
module.exports = {
  extends: ['eslint:recommended'],
  parserOptions: {
    ecmaVersion: 6,
  },
  env: {
    node: true,
  },
};
```

---

6. https://eslint.org/docs/rules/

Now give the linter one more try:

```
$ npx eslint palindromes.js
```

No output? Great! When it comes to linting, no news is good news.

Commit your work so far, using the recommended gitmoji for configuration changes:

```
:wrench: Initial ESLint setup
```

If you'd like more information on anything we've done so far, see the docs on configuring ESLint.[7] Next up, we're going to build a slightly different set of linter rules for our test file.

Extending an ESLint Configuration

ESLint is now perfectly content with palindromes.js, but if you try to run it against palindromes.test.js, it won't be so happy:

```
$ npx eslint palindromes.test.js
/Users/tburnham/code/test-driven-palindromes/palindromes.test.js
   3:1   error   'describe' is not defined   no-undef
   4:3   error   'it' is not defined         no-undef
   5:5   error   'expect' is not defined     no-undef

✖ 3 problems (3 errors, 0 warnings)
```

All of these problems share the same cause as the module kerfuffle earlier: ESLint doesn't know that palindromes.test.js will be running in an environment (Jest) where describe, it, and expect are defined as globals.

You could fix the problem with another env entry, but there's a better way. Jest has an official ESLint plugin, eslint-plugin-jest,[8] which comes with several rules for identifying common test code mistakes. Go ahead and add it to the project:

```
$ npm install --save-dev eslint-plugin-jest@22.1.2
+ eslint-plugin-jest@22.1.2
```

To apply the plugin, you need to make two changes to the ESLint configuration: first, register it in a plugins entry; and second, add its recommended configuration to the extends entry:

---

7. https://eslint.org/docs/user-guide/configuring
8. https://github.com/jest-community/eslint-plugin-jest

```
// .eslintrc.js
module.exports = {
  plugins: ['jest'],
  extends: ['eslint:recommended', 'plugin:jest/recommended'],
  parserOptions: {
    ecmaVersion: 6,
  },
  env: {
    node: true,
  },
};
```

Now you should be able to lint palindromes.test.js without complaint:

```
$ npx eslint palindromes.test.js
```

However, there is a slight problem with this setup: those Jest-specific configuration settings now apply to every JavaScript file in the project! We want one set of configuration rules for tests, and another set for everything else. The best way to accomplish that is to move the tests into their own subdirectory. There we can define a test-specific ESLint configuration that extends the more general configuration in the project root.

Remove the Jest entries by resetting the root ESLint configuration to its last committed state via VS Code's "Discard Changes" command, or from the Terminal:

```
$ git checkout -- .eslintrc.js
```

Create a new directory called tests and move palindromes.test.js into it. Change the require() path on the file's first line to correct the relative path (VS Code may have already done this for you):

```
// tests/palindromes.test.js
const palindromes = require('../palindromes');
...
```

Now remove the Jest-specific settings from the root .eslintrc.js, and add them instead to a new .eslintrc.js in the tests directory:

```
ch2/tests/.eslintrc.js
module.exports = {
  plugins: ['jest'],
  extends: ['plugin:jest/recommended'],
};
```

Every time ESLint runs against a JavaScript file, it looks for the closest configuration. Then it continues looking in all parent directories, merging all of the configurations it finds (with closer configurations given greater precedence). So when ESLint runs against tests/palindromes.test.js, it'll apply not only the Jest plugin's rules but also the "eslint: recommended" rules. The parserOptions and env will carry over as well. This inheritance pattern means we only have to make configuration changes to a single file for those rules to apply project wide.

Try it out for yourself:

```
$ npx eslint tests/palindromes.test.js
```

Once you get the all-clear, commit the new project structure using the gitmoji for moving files around:

```
:truck: Move tests into their own folder
```

Integrating ESLint with VS Code

As useful as ESLint's command-line reports are, they're less than ideal ergonomically. First, running the linter manually takes you out of the coding flow. And second, using the line and column numbers in the error report to identify the code in question is a chore. It'd be much handier to see the linter's feedback directly in your code. Happily, we can do exactly that, by adding the ESLint extension to VS Code.

Open the Extensions sidebar (^⇧X) and search for "ESLint." Several extensions will pop up. At the top of the list, you should see an extension simply named "ESLint" by Dirk Baeumer.[9] Click the green "Install" button.

Try typing something nonsensical in either of the project's JS files. Within milliseconds, your gibberish will be underlined in bright red. ESLint is linting your code as you type! Hover over the underlined code to see which linter rule you're breaking. Also notice that the scrollbar area (officially called the "overview ruler") has red squares marking the lines with red underlining—handy for scrolling directly to linter problems in large files.

VS Code tracks all problems reported by linters and aggregates them in the left corner of the status bar (next to the source control branch indicator), where you can always see the total number of errors and warnings found in all open files. Click these numbers and the Problems pane will open with a complete list, as you can see in the screenshot on page 35.

---

9. https://marketplace.visualstudio.com/items?itemName=dbaeumer.vscode-eslint

You can click any of the listed problems to jump to the corresponding point in your code. To get a feel for how all of this feedback can help, try adding another assertion to the existing test:

```
// tests/palindromes.test.js
const palindromes = require('../palindromes')

describe('palindromes()', () => {
  it('correctly identifies one-word palindromes', () => {
    expect(palindromes('madam')).toEqual(['madam']);
    expect(palindromes('racecar')).toEqual(['racecar']);
  })
});
```

Any mistake you make will trigger instant alarm bells. If, for example, you were to misplace the closing parenthesis for the expect() so that it contained the toEqual(), the linter would complain (thanks to the Jest plugin) that No assertion was called on expect().

Having linter feedback as you type is terrific for catching typos, but it also means getting a lot of false positives, as the linter is liable to complain before you've finished typing what you've intended. Many developers don't mind this, but if you'd prefer to do without the noise, you can tell the ESLint integration to wait until save via the eslint.run setting:

```
// User Settings
{
    ...
    "eslint.run": "onSave",
}
```

And that's all you need to get up and running with ESLint. We've seen how to add ESLint to a project, how to use nested configurations, and how to run the linter automatically with VS Code. In the next section, we'll take our quest for better code through better tooling even further with automated formatting.

Beautifying Code with Prettier

Prettier[10] describes itself as "an opinionated code formatter." First introduced in 2017, it's already soared to two million downloads per week from the npm registry. Using Prettier for the first time feels like a breath of fresh air: No more worrying about insignificant stylistic details as you work. No more arguments with your team about what's most readable. Just let the formatter take care of it.

Let's add Prettier to our project. Since we're using ESLint, we want the prettier-eslint command, which ensures that Prettier formats our code in a manner that's consistent with our ESLint config. To get that command, install the prettier-eslint-cli package:

```
$ npm install --save-dev prettier-eslint-cli@4.7.1
+ prettier-eslint-cli@4.7.1
```

Try running prettier-eslint against our test suite:

```
$ npx prettier-eslint tests/palindromes.test.js
const palindromes = require("../palindromes");

describe("palindromes()", () => {
  it("correctly identifies one-word palindromes", () => {
    expect(palindromes("madam")).toEqual(["madam"]);
    expect(palindromes("racecar")).toEqual(["racecar"]);
  });
});
success formatting 1 file with prettier-eslint
```

Prettier read tests/palindromes.test.js and emitted a formatted version as its output. (It didn't change the file itself.) If you typed the original code exactly as it was

---

10. https://prettier.io/

presented in the book, there's only one change in the formatted version: the strings are double-quoted rather than single-quoted, per Prettier's default configuration. Happily, if you don't like Prettier's double-quote absolutism, you have the power to change it.

Configuring Prettier

By itself, Prettier has only a handful of configuration options.[11] However, when using the prettier-eslint bridge, you can exercise finer-grained control over formatting by setting ESLint rules.

Let's say that you want to prefer single-quotes over double-quotes, except in cases where using double-quotes would avoid escaping (e.g., 'Your right' is preferable to "Your right", but "You're right" is preferable to 'You\'re right'). You can express this with the ESLint quotes rule[12] like so:

```
// .eslintrc.js
module.exports = {
  ...
  rules: {
    quotes: ['error', 'single', { avoidEscape: true }],
  },
};
```

Save the updated ESLint config file and re-run the format script against our test suite:

```
$ npx prettier-eslint tests/palindromes.test.js
...
const palindromes = require('../palindromes');

describe('palindromes()', () => {
  it('correctly identifies one-word palindromes', () => {
    expect(palindromes('madam')).toEqual(['madam']);
    expect(palindromes('racecar')).toEqual(['racecar']);
  });
});
success formatting 1 file with prettier-eslint
```

Another common piece of code style configuration is how to handle trailing commas. By default, Prettier strips away all unnecessary trailing commas. You may have noticed that the code in this book uses commas at the end of lines when those lines are object or array entries. (For example, the .eslintrc.js above exhibits this pattern.) Many JS developers prefer this style, in part because it keeps version control diffs simpler. For example, changing

---

11. https://prettier.io/docs/en/options.html
12. https://eslint.org/docs/rules/quotes

```
arr = [
  1,
  2
];
```

to

```
arr = [
  1,
  2,
  3
];
```

results in a diff that looks like this:

```
arr = [
  1,
- 2
+ 2,
+ 3
];
```

If the last array entry already had a trailing comma, then the diff would be more concise and reflective of the actual change:

```
arr = [
  1,
  2,
+ 3,
];
```

You can override this behavior by setting ESLint's comma-dangle rule[13] to always-multiline, giving us our final .eslintrc.js:

ch2/.eslintrc.js
```
module.exports = {
  extends: ['eslint:recommended'],
  parserOptions: {
    ecmaVersion: 6,
  },
  env: {
    node: true,
  },
  rules: {
    quotes: ['error', 'single', { avoidEscape: true }],
    'comma-dangle': ['error', 'always-multiline'],
  },
};
```

---

13. https://eslint.org/docs/rules/comma-dangle

Open the Source Control sidebar and commit:

```
:wrench: Initial Prettier setup
```

Integrating Prettier with VS Code

As with ESLint, Prettier works best when integrated into your editor, allowing you to format your code with a single keystroke—or, if you prefer, without you even having to ask.

Open the Extensions sidebar (^⇧X) and search for Prettier. At the top of the list you should see an extension named "Prettier" by Esben Petersen.[14] Click the green "Install" button.

Prettier is what's known as a "formatter extension." When you run the "Format Document" command (⇧⌥F), VS Code checks the installed extensions to see if any of them wants to perform formatting on the given document. Open up, say, tests/palindromes.test.js, and run that command now.

Running the formatter changed the single-quotes to double-quotes! That's because the Prettier extension automatically reads the Prettier configuration from your project, but it doesn't automatically detect the ESLint bridge. For that, you will need to change a setting. Let's open up User Settings and add this line:

```
// User Settings
{
    ...
    "prettier.eslintIntegration": true,
}
```

Now try formatting tests/palindromes.test.js again. The double-quotes should go back to single-quotes, as expected. Save the file and confirm that the results of running the format script match up with the results of running "Format Document" in the editor:

```
$ npx prettier-eslint tests/palindromes.test.js
...
1 file was unchanged
```

As handy as the "Format Document" command is, we can do better. Open the project's Workspace Settings and add one final customization, editor.formatOnSave:

---

14. https://marketplace.visualstudio.com/items?itemName=esbenp.prettier-vscode

```
ch2/.vscode/settings.json
{
  "files.exclude": {
      "node_modules": true,
      "package-lock.json": true
  },
  "[javascript]": {
      "editor.tabSize": 2
  },
  "editor.formatOnSave": true
}
```

The editor.formatOnSave flag does just what it sounds like, running "Format Document" for you every time you save a file. Try it now: open up a few files in the project, make tweaks, hit save, and watch them instantly change. Achieving consistent formatting has never been easier!

If you're feeling adventurous (or impatient), there's an editor.formatOnType flag, too. Most developers find this mode too jarring, but if you have a taste for fast feedback, it's worth trying out.

Adding Project Lint Scripts

You've learned how to run ESLint and Prettier from the command line with npx, and directly from your editor. But that knowledge is locked inside your head! To make your project more approachable to potential collaborators, it's a good idea to include some linting scripts in package.json.

Here we have a lint script that tests all JS files for lints and formatting issues, and a format script that runs all JS files through Prettier and overwrites the originals:

```
ch2/package.json
{
  "name": "test-driven-palindromes",
  "private": true,
  "version": "1.0.0",
  "description": "",
  "main": "index.js",
  "scripts": {
    "test": "jest",
    "lint": "eslint . && prettier-eslint --list-different **/*.js",
    "format": "prettier-eslint --write **/*.js"
  },
  "keywords": [],
  "author": "",
  "license": "ISC",
```

```
  "devDependencies": {
    "eslint": "^5.10.0",
    "eslint-plugin-jest": "^22.1.2",
    "jest": "^23.6.0",
    "prettier-eslint-cli": "^4.7.1"
  }
}
```

❶ To run against every JS file in the project, ESLint only needs the . argument, indicating the project directory. Prettier is a little more demanding, requiring a glob. The --list-different flag tells Prettier to list the names of any files with formatting issues, rather than emitting their formatted contents.

If you run these scripts, you should see some nice, boring output, since your code is already pretty:

```
$ npm run format
...
2 files were unchanged
```

Later on, in Chapter 6, Continuous Integration and Collaboration, on page 147, you'll learn to use these scripts to enforce your code style standards automatically.

That concludes our introduction to Prettier. We've seen how to add Prettier to a project, how the prettier-eslint bridge lets us use ESLint rules to modify Prettier's output, and how editor integration makes formatting with Prettier an effortless process.

In the next section, you'll meet this chapter's final piece of tooling: Wallaby.

Real-Time Testing with Wallaby

Imagine a world where there are no boundaries between your code and your tests. Instead of saving changes to your code and seeing the output from Jest in a separate panel, you would see the results of your tests instantly as you type, right before your eyes. Code with passing tests would be marked with a reassuring green. Code with failing tests would be highlighted in red, with a description of the failure floating next to it. Sounds like magic? It's real, and it's called Wallaby.

In addition to working like magic, Wallaby is a commercial product. We JavaScript developers have been blessed (spoiled, some would say) by an abundance of free tools. All of the other amazing software I've mentioned in this chapter—VS Code, Jest, ESLint, Prettier—is free and open source. But there is, quite simply, nothing else like Wallaby. There's a 30-day free trial, so don't let the price tag deter you from following along with this chapter.

Open up the Extensions sidebar, search for "Wallaby.js," and install. A notification will pop up in the corner:

> Installing wallaby.js dependencies. It may take a minute or two, you will be notified once the install is finished.

While that's happening, we can configure Wallaby for our project. Create a file called wallaby.js at the root of the project:

```
ch2/wallaby.js
module.exports = function() {
  return {
    testFramework: 'jest',

    env: {
      type: 'node',
    },

    tests: ['tests/**/*.test.js'],
    files: ['**/*.js', '!node_modules/**/*', '!**/*.test.js', '!**/.*'],
  };
};
```

❶ testFramework: 'jest' is pretty self-explanatory: It tells Wallaby to use Jest to run our tests, as opposed to another framework like Jasmine or Mocha.

❷ env.type: 'node' tells Wallaby to run our tests in Node, as opposed to a browser environment.

❸ tests: ['tests/**/*.test.js'] tells Wallaby where to find the test files in this project.

❹ files: ['**/*.js', '!node_modules/**/*', '!**/*.test.js', '!**/.*'] tells Wallaby where to find the project's source files. The patterns preceded by ! are excluded, preventing Wallaby from trying to treat JS files in node_modules, or ending in .test.js, or starting with . (like .eslintrc.js) as source files.

Why does Wallaby need to know where to find all of the source files in the project? Because Wallaby caches its own copies of these files in memory, allowing it to re-run tests in the blink of an eye.

Once Wallaby's dependencies are installed and our configuration is saved, run "Wallaby.js: Start" from the Command Palette. You'll be prompted to select a configuration file; use the one we just created. Wallaby may take a while to initialize for the first time, so go get yourself a cup of coffee. When you get back, your workspace should resemble the screenshot on page 43.

Notice that there's now an indicator near the lower-right corner of the screen that shows the number of passing and failing tests. More strikingly, there are several green annotations next to lines in both palindromes.js and palindromes.test.js.

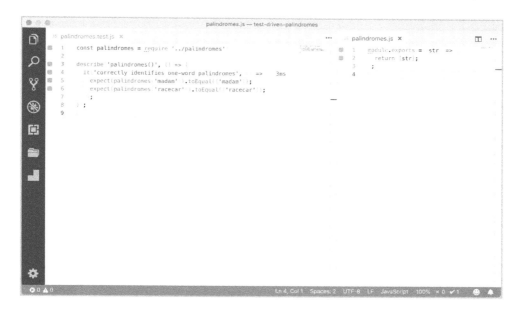

The annotations are Wallaby's magic sauce. When a line has a green annotation, that means that the line is covered by your tests. If every line in your project's source code has a green annotation, then congrats: you've achieved 100% code coverage!

Try changing the second line of the test to make it fail. Within milliseconds, Wallaby reruns the tests. The failing test line now has a red annotation, meaning that it throws an error (as expect() does when it fails). The specific error is shown next to that line. You can see a full readout with Wallaby's "Show Failing Tests" command, as shown in the screenshot on page 44.

Notice that the passing test line has a pink annotation, as does the function body in palindromes.js. The pink annotation means that the line is in the execution path of a failing test. This is an incredibly useful aid for tracking down the cause of test failures, as you can rule out all lines not marked in pink as irrelevant.

Wallaby also has a grey annotation for lines that are not covered by tests, and a yellow annotation for lines that are only partly covered by tests.

Seeing your code so liberally decorated may take some getting used to, but once you do, you'll find the information Wallaby provides invaluable. Wallaby is both the fastest way to run your tests and the most thorough results reporter.

A Wallaby Challenge

With Wallaby at the ready, have a go at using TDD to implement the palindrome finder features described by these tests:

```
it('returns an empty array when given no palindromes', () => {
  expect(palindromes('tic tac toe')).toEqual([]);
});

it('ignores casing', () => {
  expect(palindromes('WoW')).toEqual(['wow']);
});

it('ignores punctuation', () => {
  expect(palindromes('yo, banana boy!')).toEqual(['yobananaboy']);
});

it('detects multi-word palindromes', () => {
  expect(palindromes('A man, a plan, a canal, Panama')).toEqual([
    'amanaplanacanalpanama',
  ]);
});
```

This is intended to be a challenge, so don't expect it to be as easy as Fizz Buzz. The important thing is that you learn to take advantage of the real-time feedback provided by Wallaby and the other tools introduced earlier as you work. Be sure to add tests for any utility functions you might write along the way. You can find an example solution at the end of the chapter.

Mantra: Live in the Code

Every time your eyes leave your code, you experience what's known as a context switch. Returning to your code, it's common to feel disoriented, even lost. A TDD workflow that requires you to actively switch between your code and your tests will sap your ability to focus. Hence this chapter's mantra: *"live in the code."* Strive to make running your tests as automatic as breathing.

This chapter introduced you to the VS Code editor, a powerful and endlessly customizable home for your TDD workflow. You learned to use ESLint to preemptively avoid common coding mistakes that tests might miss, and to use Prettier to keep your code tidy without losing your momentum. Finally, you tried out Wallaby, which takes TDD to the next level by running your tests continuously as you type and drawing your attention to the code involved with every failure.

In the next chapter, you'll apply these tools to the challenge of writing React components.

Example Palindrome Finder Solution

ch2/tests/palindromes.test.js
```javascript
const palindromes = require('../palindromes');
const { prepareStr, isPalindrome, stringStartPalindrome } = palindromes;

describe('prepareStr()', () => {
  it('converts the given string to lowercase', () => {
    expect(prepareStr('aAaA')).toBe('aaaa');
  });

  it('removes all non-letter characters', () => {
    expect(
      prepareStr('To infinity, and beyond!')
    ).toBe('toinfinityandbeyond');
  });
});

describe('isPalindrome()', () => {
  it('returns true when given a palindrome', () => {
    expect(isPalindrome('aba')).toBe(true);
    expect(isPalindrome('abba')).toBe(true);
  });

  it('returns false when given a non-palindrome', () => {
    expect(isPalindrome('abb')).toBe(false);
    expect(isPalindrome('aaba')).toBe(false);
  });
});

describe('stringStartPalindrome()', () => {
  it('returns the longest palindrome at the start of the string', () => {
    expect(stringStartPalindrome('wow')).toBe('wow');
    expect(stringStartPalindrome('ahha')).toBe('ahha');
    expect(stringStartPalindrome('hohoho')).toBe('hohoh');
  });

  it('returns null if no length 3+ palindrome starts the string', () => {
    expect(stringStartPalindrome('ww')).toBe(null);
    expect(stringStartPalindrome('abcda')).toBe(null);
    expect(stringStartPalindrome('bananarama')).toBe(null);
  });
});

describe('palindromes()', () => {
  it('correctly identifies one-word palindromes', () => {
    expect(palindromes('madam')).toEqual(['madam']);
    expect(palindromes('racecar')).toEqual(['racecar']);
  });

  it('returns an empty array when given no palindromes', () => {
    expect(palindromes('tic tac toe')).toEqual([]);
  });
```

```
  it('ignores casing', () => {
    expect(palindromes('WoW')).toEqual(['wow']);
  });

  it('ignores punctuation', () => {
    expect(palindromes('yo, banana boy!')).toEqual(['yobananaboy']);
  });

  it('detects multi-word palindromes', () => {
    expect(palindromes('A man, a plan, a canal, Panama')).toEqual([
      'amanaplanacanalpanama',
    ]);
  });
});
```

ch2/palindromes.js
```
const prepareStr = str => str.toLowerCase().replace(/[^a-z]/g, '');

const isPalindrome = str => {
  const endIndex = str.length - 1;
  for (let i = 0; i < str.length / 2; i++) {
    if (str[i] !== str[endIndex - i]) return false;
  }
  return true;
};

const stringStartPalindrome = str => {
  const firstLetter = str[0];
  let lastIndex = str.lastIndexOf(firstLetter);
  while (lastIndex >= 2) {
    const candidate = str.substring(0, lastIndex + 1);
    if (isPalindrome(candidate)) {
      return candidate;
    }
    lastIndex = str.lastIndexOf(firstLetter, lastIndex - 1);
  }
  return null;
};

const palindromes = str => {
  const matches = [];
  let startIndex = 0;
  str = prepareStr(str);
  while (startIndex < str.length / 2) {
    const palindrome = stringStartPalindrome(str.substring(startIndex));
    if (palindrome) {
      matches.push(palindrome);
      startIndex += palindrome.length;
    } else {
      startIndex++;
    }
  }
```

```
  return matches;
};

// Attach helpers to the exported function for testing
palindromes.prepareStr = prepareStr;
palindromes.isPalindrome = isPalindrome;
palindromes.stringStartPalindrome = stringStartPalindrome;

module.exports = palindromes;
```

CHAPTER 3

Testing React with Enzyme

JavaScript web development can be divided into two eras: pre-React and post-React. Pre-React, all was chaos. Suppose you wanted to make a button toggle a popup when clicked: you'd add code *somewhere*—nowhere near the button markup—to add an event listener for the button click. The event listener you'd write would directly alter the DOM to show or hide the popup. Code was scattered without rhyme or reason. Unit tests were almost unheard of.

Thankfully, we live in the age of React. Now individual pieces of the app—the button and the popover, in this example—can be isolated as *components*. The DOM tree they render is a pure function of their *props* (React parlance for data provided to the component) and their internal state. And that purity makes them a breeze to test.

In this chapter, you'll use a test-driven approach to build a complex component one piece at a time. You'll use the Babel compiler to incorporate React's powerful JSX syntax into your tests. You'll combine the speed of Jest with the ease of Enzyme, a harness that lets you test individual React components in isolation. Along the way, you'll take advantage of the tools introduced in the previous chapter, applying them to a cutting-edge React stack.

Starting a React Project

Our project for this chapter, and for the remainder of the book, will be a carousel component. Carousels have become ubiquitous on the web, yet many implementations fall short in various ways. By building your own, you'll be able to adapt it to your project's needs.

Create a new directory called test-driven-carousel and opening it in VS Code:

```
$ mkdir test-driven-carousel/
$ code test-driven-carousel/
```

Use VS Code's "Git: Initialize Repository" command, or run

```
$ git init
```

on the command line. Once the repo is initialized, add the .gitignore from the previous chapter:

```
ch3/.gitignore
node_modules/
.vscode/
```

Then create a package.json using npm:

```
$ npm init -y
```

As in the previous chapters, add a "private": true entry to the package.json to silence various npm warnings:

```
// package.json
{
  "name": "test-driven-carousel",
  "private": true,
  "version": "1.0.0",
  "description": "",
  "main": "index.js",
  "scripts": {
    "test": "echo \"Error: no test specified\" && exit 1"
  },
  "keywords": [],
  "author": "",
  "license": "ISC"
}
```

With those two core files in place, make an initial commit:

```
:tada: First commit
```

So far, so familiar. Next, we'll move into new territory as we add support for a little language called JSX.

Saving Time with Boilerplate Projects

In this book, you set up each project from scratch so that you can understand what each piece of tooling is doing and how you can modify it to your liking. However, if you're starting a new project on your own and don't mind a little mystery, you might want to try a React boilerplate, such as Facebook's own create-react-app.[a] It'll handle the configuration for you, so you can jump right into writing React code.

---

a.   https://github.com/facebook/create-react-app/

Using Babel for JSX

Like any other JavaScript library, React is fully usable through plain, ordinary JavaScript code. But hardly anyone uses it that way. Instead, they compile a language called *JSX* down to ordinary JavaScript.

JSX allows HTML-like markup to be embedded within JavaScript code. Every tag in JSX is converted to a call to React.createElement(). So for instance, the code

```
const helloJSX = <h1 className="super-big">Hello, JSX!</h1>;
```

would be compiled to

```
const helloJSX = React.createElement(
  'h1',
  { className: 'super-big' },
  'Hello, JSX!'
);
```

If you're new to JSX, this new syntax will take some getting used to. But it makes code much easier to read and write than the equivalent series of React.createElement() calls would be. For more details on JSX syntax, take a look at the React docs.[1]

The compiler that translates JSX into ordinary JavaScript is known as Babel.[2] And it does so much more than just JSX: with Babel, you can write code that uses JavaScript features from the future—those that are only implemented in leading-edge browsers—and run that code *everywhere*. More precisely, you can run that code in any JavaScript environment that supports the ECMAScript 5 standard (2009). Remember Internet Explorer 9? Yep: thanks to Babel, it can run React code!

An Ode to CoffeeScript

My first book was on CoffeeScript, a language introduced by Jeremy Ashkenas in 2009 as "a little language that compiles into JavaScript." CoffeeScript was hugely influential in two respects: first, it pioneered a number of syntax features that would make their way into the ECMAScript 6 standard; and second, it was the first compile-to-JavaScript language to catch on. The success of CoffeeScript sparked widespread interest in ES6-to-ES5 compilers, which is how Babel came to be.

CoffeeScript's time has passed, but today's JavaScripters may have it to thank for kicking off an era of innovation for the once stagnant language. I'm proud to have played a small role in bringing it to the world's attention.

---

1. https://reactjs.org/docs/introducing-jsx.html
2. https://babeljs.io/

To start using Babel, add its core package to the project:

```
$ npm install --save-dev @babel/core@7.2.0
+ @babel/core@7.2.0
```

As with ESLint, Babel requires some configuration to make it useful. For this project, you'll start with two popular Babel presets:

- The React preset,[3] which provides support for JSX.
- The env preset,[4] which provides support for all new JavaScript syntax features defined in ES2015 (a.k.a. ES6), ES2016, and ES2017. The name "env" refers to its ability to tailor the transpilation pipeline to a specified set of target environments.

Install the presets with npm:

```
$ npm install --save-dev @babel/preset-react@7.0.0 @babel/preset-env@7.2.0
+ @babel/preset-react@7.0.0
+ @babel/preset-env@7.2.0
```

Then bring in the two presets from a new file called .babelrc.js:

```
// .babelrc.js
module.exports = {
  presets: ['@babel/preset-react', '@babel/preset-env'],
};
```

Babel will now apply this configuration to every JS file in the project. To try it out, create a JS file called hello-babel.js:

```
// hello-babel.js
import figlet from 'figlet';
console.log(figlet.textSync('Hello, Babel!'));
```

This file uses the ES2015 modules syntax in the form of the import keyword. If you try running it in Node without Babel, you'll get a syntax error:

```
$ node hello-babel.js
/Users/tburnham/code/test-driven-carousel/hello-babel.js:1
(function (exports, require, module, __filename, __dirname) {
    import figlet from 'figlet';
    ^^^^^^

SyntaxError: Unexpected token import
    at createScript (vm.js:80:10)
    at Object.runInThisContext (vm.js:139:10)
    at Module._compile (module.js:616:28)
    at Object.Module._extensions..js (module.js:663:10)
```

---

3.   https://babeljs.io/docs/en/babel-preset-react
4.   https://babeljs.io/docs/en/babel-preset-env

```
  at Module.load (module.js:565:32)
  at tryModuleLoad (module.js:505:12)
  at Function.Module._load (module.js:497:3)
  at Function.Module.runMain (module.js:693:10)
  at startup (bootstrap_node.js:191:16)
  at bootstrap_node.js:612:3
```

To run this file through Babel from the command line, you will need the @babel/cli package:

```
$ npm install @babel/cli@7.2.0
+ @babel/cli@7.2.0
```

@babel/cli includes an executable called babel that you can run with npx:

```
$ npx babel hello-babel.js
"use strict";

var _figlet = _interopRequireDefault(require("figlet"));

function _interopRequireDefault(obj) {
  return obj && obj.__esModule ? obj : { default: obj };
}

console.log(_figlet.default.textSync('Hello, Babel!'));
```

You don't need to understand the details of this code. Long story short, Babel has compiled the import syntax into something that's compatible with Node and other environments that don't support ES2015 modules.

You can run the compiled script by piping it into node. But first, install that package it's trying to import:

```
$ npm install figlet@1.2.0
+ figlet@1.2.0
```

Now check out what happens:

```
$ npx babel hello-babel.js | node
```

Figlet[5] took a plain old string and turned it into ASCII art. Pretty cool!

You can clean up hello-babel.js and its dependencies, as we won't need them:

```
$ rm hello-babel.js
$ npm uninstall @babel/cli figlet
```

---

5.   https://github.com/patorjk/figlet.js

Then commit the new .babelrc.js and the changes to package.json:

```
:wrench: Initial Babel setup
```

In the next section, we'll use the power of Babel to bring exciting new syntax features to the world of Jest testing.

Bridging Jest and Babel

Let's bring Jest to the party. In order to get Jest to run tests through Babel, you'll need both jest and a package called babel-jest:

```
$ npm install --save-dev jest@23.6.0 babel-jest@23.6.0
+ jest@23.6.0
+ babel-jest@23.6.0
```

As of this writing, you'll also need a special version of the babel-core package. The reason is that the package recently switched names: Babel 6 called it babel-core, but Babel 7 namespaces it as @babel/core. So this package creates a bridge for projects looking for babel-core to direct them to @babel/core:

```
$ npm install --save-dev babel-core@^7.0.0-bridge.0
+ babel-core@^7.0.0-bridge.0
```

Next, update the scripts entry in package.json to make Jest the project's official test runner:

```
// package.json
{
  ...
  "scripts": {
    "test": "jest"
  },
  ...
}
```

And since you will be writing React components, naturally you will need the react package:

```
$ npm install react@16.4.2
+ react@16.4.2
```

Notice that this is the first time in the book that we've omitted --save-dev when installing a dependency. Since React will be used at runtime in our app (remember, those JSX tags compile to React.createElement() calls!), it's not just a development dependency.

You'll also need the react-dom package, a bridge between React elements and the DOM, though only as a dev dependency for testing:

```
$ npm install --save-dev react-dom@16.4.2
+ react-dom@16.4.2
```

Create a test file that takes advantage of JSX and the ES2015 import syntax:

```
// src/tests/hello.test.js
import React from 'react';

describe('JSX', () => {
  it('calls React.createElement', () => {
    const createElementSpy = jest.spyOn(React, 'createElement');
    <h1>Hello, JSX!</h1>;
    expect(createElementSpy).toHaveBeenCalledWith('h1', null, 'Hello, JSX!');
  });
});
```

❶ jest.spyOn(React, "createElement") replaces the React.createElement() method with a spy that intercepts calls, allowing us to make assertions about how that method is used.

❷ expect(spy).toHaveBeenCalledWith() does just what it says on the tin, failing if the spy wasn't called or was called with a different set of arguments.

Give it a try:

```
$ npx jest
 PASS  hello.test.js
  JSX
    ✓ calls React.createElement (5ms)

Test Suites: 1 passed, 1 total
Tests:       1 passed, 1 total
Snapshots:   0 total
Time:        1.373s
Ran all test suites.
```

Huzzah! Jest automatically recognized Babel and ran our test file through it before running it. Commit the configuration change:

```
:wrench: Initial Jest setup
```

Next, we'll bring the ever-helpful ESLint and Prettier into the land of Babel.

Adding ESLint and Prettier

To get this new project linted, start by installing some deps that were introduced in the previous chapter:

```
$ npm install --save-dev eslint@5.10.0 \
    prettier-eslint-cli@4.7.1 \
    eslint-plugin-jest@22.1.2
+ eslint@5.10.0
+ prettier-eslint-cli@4.7.1
+ eslint-plugin-jest@22.1.2
```

Then add the scripts from last chapter's package.json:

```
// package.json
{
  ...
  "scripts": {
    "test": "jest",
    "lint": "eslint . && prettier-eslint --list-different **/*.js",
    "format": "prettier-eslint --write **/*.js"
  },
  ...
}
```

We'll use three nested ESLint configurations for this project:

1. The root configuration, .eslintrc.js
2. The source configuration, src/.eslintrc.js
3. The test configuration, src/tests/.eslintrc.js

The root and test configurations are borrowed from last chapter's project:

```
// .eslintrc.js
module.exports = {
  extends: ['eslint:recommended'],
  parserOptions: {
    ecmaVersion: 6,
  },
  env: {
    node: true,
  },
  rules: {
    quotes: ['error', 'single', { avoidEscape: true }],
    'comma-dangle': ['error', 'always-multiline'],
  },
};
```

ch3/src/tests/.eslintrc.js
```
module.exports = {
  plugins: ['jest'],
  extends: ['plugin:jest/recommended'],
};
```

The new configuration in src tells ESLint that our project's code is intended for a browser environment:

ch3/src/.eslintrc.js
```
module.exports = {
  env: {
    browser: true,
  },
};
```

Then try out the linter on our test file:

```
$ npx eslint src/tests/hello.test.js
...
/Users/tburnham/code/test-driven-carousel/src/tests/hello.test.js
  1:1  error  Parsing error: 'import' and 'export' may appear only with
    'sourceType: module'

✖ 1 problem (1 error, 0 warnings)
```

The error indicates that ESLint is aware of the import syntax but isn't sure if this JS file is supposed to be an ES2015 module. For this project, we want all JS files to be ES2015 modules. To get ESLint to recognize them as such, modify the parserOptions in the root ESLint config:

```
// .eslintrc.js
module.exports = {
  ...
➤  parserOptions: {
➤    ecmaVersion: 6,
❶    sourceType: 'module',
➤  },
  ...
};
```

❶ sourceType: 'module' tells ESLint that our code will run in an environment that supports the ES2015 (a.k.a. ES6) import/export syntax.

Try running the linter again:

```
$ npx eslint src/tests/hello.test.js
...
/Users/tburnham/code/test-driven-carousel/src/tests/hello.test.js
  6:5  error  Parsing error: Unexpected token <

✘ 1 problem (1 error, 0 warnings)
```

Now ESLint is saying that it doesn't recognize JSX syntax. This, too, is best solved through parserOptions:

```
// .eslintrc.js
module.exports = {
  ...
➤ parserOptions: {
➤   ecmaVersion: 6,
➤   sourceType: 'module',
➤   ecmaFeatures: {
➤     jsx: true,
➤   },
➤ },
  ...
};
```

One more attempt:

```
$ npx eslint src/tests/hello.test.js
```

No news from ESLint is good news! Since you'll be using React in your tests, it's a good idea to make the linter aware of it. To do that, you'll need another plugin, eslint-plugin-react:[6]

```
$ npm install --save-dev eslint-plugin-react@7.11.1
+ eslint-plugin-react@7.11.1
```

Apply the plugin by adding it to the plugins section of your ESLint config, then add its recommended set of rules to our extends list. This plugin is relevant to app code as well as tests, so it belongs in the root ESLint config:

```
// .eslintrc.js
module.exports = {
➤ plugins: ['react'],
➤ extends: ['eslint:recommended', 'plugin:react/recommended'],
  ...
};
```

The set of recommended rules is designed to catch a number of common React coding mistakes. Additionally, eslint-plugin-react can make suggestions targeted to the React version you're using if you specify it in a settings block:

---

6. https://github.com/yannickcr/eslint-plugin-react

```
// .eslintrc.js
module.exports = {
  ...
➤  settings: {
➤    react: {
➤      version: '16.4.2',
➤    },
➤  },
};
```

What about Prettier? If you're using VS Code, try running the Format Document command on the test file. If you're using another editor, use the command npx prettier-eslint --write src/tests/hello.test.js. Either way, the file should run through Prettier without complaint. Thanks to the prettier-eslint bridge, it knows all about the special syntax features that we've told ESLint to recognize.

If you're using VS Code and want to run Prettier on save, this would be a good time to enable editor.formatOnSave for this project. In fact, all of the Workspace Settings from last chapter's project are appropriate for this project:

ch3/.vscode/settings.json
```
{
  "files.exclude": {
      "node_modules": true,
      "package-lock.json": true
  },
  "[javascript]": {
      "editor.tabSize": 2
  },
  "editor.formatOnSave": true
}
```

Now it's time to make another commit:

:wrench: Initial ESLint and Prettier config

Add one last supporting technology before we switch into TDD mode: Wallaby.

Configuring Wallaby for Babel

In order to get Wallaby up and running, we need to make some changes to our config from the last chapter. If you're not using Wallaby, start Jest in watch mode (npx jest --watchAll) and skip ahead to the next section.

Create a new wallaby.js file in the root of the project:

ch3/wallaby.js
```
module.exports = function(wallaby) {
  return {
    testFramework: 'jest',
```

```
    env: {
      type: 'node',
    },
    tests: ['src/tests/**/*.test.js'],
    files: ['src/**/*.js', '!**/*.test.js', '!**/.*'],
    compilers: {
❶      '**/*.js': wallaby.compilers.babel(),
    },
  };
};
```

❶ The compilers entry tells Wallaby that all .js files should be compiled with Babel.

Run the Wallaby.js: Start command. Give it a minute to spin up, and watch as hello.test.js is bedecked in beautiful green annotations.

This calls for a commit:

```
:wrench: Initial Wallaby setup
```

Now we're ready to build our first test-driven React component!

Testing Simple Components with Enzyme

As our project for the rest of the book, we're going to build a carousel. A carousel is a widget that shows a series of images to the user one at a time. The user has the ability to move between adjacent images in the series. The carousel can also auto-advance, like a slideshow. By the end of the book, our carousel will look like this:

Seattle Photo by Ganapathy Kumar on Unsplash

Prev   Next

Since this is fairly complex, we're going to implement it as a primary component called Carousel with two secondary components:

1. CarouselSlide, an image shown in the carousel
2. CarouselButton, a button that lets the user control the slides

Let's start by writing some tests for the simplest component: CarouselButton is just going to render a <button>. (Why componentize it at all? Because we're going to add styling to that <button> in the next chapter.) We'll make assertions about the component using a library called Enzyme.

Getting Started with Enzyme

Airbnb's Enzyme has become the most popular library for testing React components. Enzyme is especially good at rendering a single component in isolation, a technique known as "shallow rendering," and letting you see how changes in the component's props and state cause its render tree to change. With shallow rendering, other components in the render tree are treated as black boxes: you can see what props they receive, but not their output. We'll be using shallow rendering for all of the React component tests in this book.

Enzyme vs. react-testing-library

As this book was written, a solid competitor to Enzyme emerged and gained traction: react-testing-library.[a] Whereas Enzyme is a Swiss Army knife for testing React components, react-testing-library is focused on a single approach: rendering components to the DOM and making assertions about that DOM tree.

Both Enzyme and react-testing-library have their pros and cons. This book advocates testing individual components in isolation, which isn't possible with react-testing-library. However, react-testing-library's approach is more conceptually straightforward. Furthermore, Enzyme's development has lagged somewhat; as of this writing, its shallow rendering mode lacks support for some cutting-edge React features, such as the new context API introduced in React 16.3.

If you're starting a new React project, do your research. Take a close look at both Enzyme and react-testing-library and decide which is the best fit for you.

---

a.   https://github.com/kentcdodds/react-testing-library

You'll need to install Enzyme, plus the "adapter" that lets it plug into the version of React you're using:

```
$ npm install --save-dev enzyme@3.8.0 enzyme-adapter-react-16@1.7.1
+ enzyme@3.8.0
+ enzyme-adapter-react-16@1.7.1
```

Delete the hello.test.js file. Then create a quick implementation of CarouselButton:

```
// src/CarouselButton.js
import React from 'react';

const CarouselButton = () => <button />;

export default CarouselButton;
```

CarouselButton is defined as a function that returns an empty <button>. Simple as it is, this is a valid React component. Note the use of capitalization: JSX treats <Uppercase /> as an instance of a *component* named Uppercase, and <lowercase /> as an instance of a *DOM element* named lowercase.

Now put this test in place:

```
// src/tests/CarouselButton.test.js
import React from 'react';
import { configure, shallow } from 'enzyme';
import Adapter from 'enzyme-adapter-react-16';
import CarouselButton from '../CarouselButton';

configure({ adapter: new Adapter() });

describe('CarouselButton', () => {
  it('renders a <button>', () => {
    const wrapper = shallow(<CarouselButton />);
    expect(wrapper.type()).toBe('button');
  });
});
```

❶ Even though our code never references React directly, we need to import it in both the component module and the test module because both use JSX expressions, which compile to React.createElement statements.

❷ Enzyme needs us to pass a React version-appropriate adapter to its configure function before we can use it, so we do that at the top of the test file. Later in this chapter, we'll move that setup code elsewhere to avoid duplicating it across all test files.

❸ Enzyme's shallow() method returns a shallow wrapper.[7]

If you run Jest, the test output should be all-green. However, savvy React developers will notice that this isn't a very useful CarouselButton implementation yet—there's no way to put content inside of the <button />! So let's get into full TDD mode, after we commit using the gitmoji for a work in progress:

```
:construction: Starting work on CarouselButton
```

---

7. https://github.com/airbnb/enzyme/blob/master/docs/api/shallow.md

Working with Props

Currently, CarouselButton renders an empty <button> element, which isn't very useful. We need to add support for setting the children of the <button> element, which will be the text that the user sees. Add a test for that to the existing describe() block:

```
// src/tests/CarouselButton.test.js
...
it('passes `children` through to the <button>', () => {
  const text = 'Button text';
  const wrapper = shallow(<CarouselButton>{text}</CarouselButton>);
  expect(wrapper.prop('children')).toBe(text);
});
...
```

The wrapper.prop(propName) method returns the value of the prop with the given name. Remember that wrapper, in this case, represents the <button> rendered by CarouselButton. Currently that button is rendered without children, failing the test. To fix that, add some prop-passing logic to the component:

```
// src/CarouselButton.js
...
const CarouselButton = ({ children }) => <button>{children}</button>;
...
```

When a component is defined as a function, that function receives the component instance's props object as the first argument. The argument list ({ children }) uses ES6's destructuring syntax to extract props.children as children, which is then passed through to the rendered <button>. Any other props are ignored.

One subtle point here: the JSX code

```
<div>{children}</div>
```

is equivalent to

```
<div children={children} />
```

That is, anything inserted between an opening tag and a closing tag is treated as that element's children prop in JSX. (If children is set in both places, the value between the tags has precedence.)

With that component change, your tests should be in the green! However, the linter isn't happy:

```
'children' is missing in props validation (react/prop-types)
```

Since you're using the recommended ESLint config from the React plugin, you're going to see a lot of constructive criticism like this. In this case, it wants you to use propTypes to declare what type of prop children is. propTypes serve two purposes. First, they're useful for documentation. Just looking at a component's propTypes often gives a good sense of its feature set. Second, they provide validation when React is running in development mode. If, for instance, you declared that children had to be a React element and a developer passed in a string instead, that developer would get a console warning.

To declare propTypes, you'll need a package called prop-types:

```
$ npm install prop-types@15.7.2
+ prop-types@15.7.2
```

Then import that package and attach a propTypes object to the component:

```
// src/CarouselButton.js
import React from 'react';
➤ import PropTypes from 'prop-types';

const CarouselButton = ({ children }) => <button>{children}</button>;

➤ CarouselButton.propTypes = {
❶   children: PropTypes.node.isRequired,
➤ };

export default CarouselButton;
```

❶ The node type means that children can be either a React element or a primitive, such as a string. And since we can reasonably expect every button to have children, it's marked as isRequired, meaning that null and undefined values are unacceptable. Prop types are strictly a development aid, and are ignored by React in production mode. You can learn more from the React docs.[8]

If you run Jest from the console, you'll notice that there's a console error, though it doesn't affect the results:

```
$ npx jest
 PASS  src/tests/CarouselButton.test.js
  CarouselButton
    ✓ renders a <button> (8ms)
    ✓ passes `children` through to the <button> (1ms)

  console.error node_modules/prop-types/checkPropTypes.js:19
    Warning: Failed prop type: The prop `children` is marked as required in
    `CarouselButton`, but its value is `undefined`.
        in CarouselButton
```

---

8.   https://reactjs.org/docs/typechecking-with-proptypes.html

```
Test Suites: 1 passed, 1 total
Tests:       2 passed, 2 total
Snapshots:   0 total
Time:        1.116s
Ran all test suites.
```

It's a good idea to always provide required props in tests, to better reflect realistic component usage. So let's provide children to the CarouselButton element in both tests. To avoid duplication, extract the shallow wrapper creation logic to a separate block called beforeEach():

```
// src/tests/CarouselButton.test.js
...
describe('CarouselButton', () => {
  const text = 'Button text';
  let wrapper;

  beforeEach(() => {
    wrapper = shallow(<CarouselButton>{text}</CarouselButton>);
  });

  it('renders a <button>', () => {
    expect(wrapper.type()).toBe('button');
  });

  it('passes `children` through to the <button>', () => {
    expect(wrapper.prop('children')).toBe(text);
  });
});
```

❶ beforeEach() executes before each test in the parent describe() block. Since there are two tests, beforeEach() will execute twice, producing two independent instances of wrapper. Giving each test its own wrapper instance ensures that no tests fail due to changes an earlier test made to its wrapper.

Now that the console error is gone, let's think ahead to what other functionality CarouselButton needs to support. In addition to passing children through to the button, we'll want to support passing an onClick event handler through. We'll also want to support passing a className prop through for styling. And we'll want to support data- attributes, too. Come to think of it, what if we just pass *every* prop through?

This is actually a very common practice in React, and a sensible one. Add another test to the existing describe() block with more prop assertions:

```
// src/tests/CarouselButton.test.js
...
it('passes other props through to the <button>', () => {
  const onClick = () => {};
  const className = 'my-carousel-button';
  const dataAction = 'prev';
  wrapper.setProps({ onClick, className, 'data-action': dataAction });
  expect(wrapper.prop('onClick')).toBe(onClick);
  expect(wrapper.prop('className')).toBe(className);
  expect(wrapper.prop('data-action')).toBe(dataAction);
});
...
```

❶ wrapper.setProps(props) simulates props being passed into the wrapped React element after the initial render, making it useful for testing lifecycle methods like componentWillReceiveProps() and componentDidUpdate(). The props passed in with setProps() are merged into the existing props object.

To satisfy the new test, update CarouselButton to pass all props through:

ch3/src/CarouselButton.js
```
import React from 'react';
import PropTypes from 'prop-types';

const CarouselButton = props => <button {...props} />;

CarouselButton.propTypes = {
  children: PropTypes.node.isRequired,
};

export default CarouselButton;
```

❶ {...props} is the JSX spread operator. It's equivalent to passing each prop in the props object through individually. That includes children, since the tag itself has no children.

By the way, now that children is no longer referenced directly, ESLint no longer requires a propTypes declaration for children. Even so, let's keep the declaration in place. It's a useful reminder that the <button> should always have text.

And we're back in the green! This is a good point for a commit:

```
:sparkles: Initial implementation of CarouselButton
```

Next, we will clear out the Enzyme configuration boilerplate from the top of the test file.

Adding a Jest Setup File

Since this chapter's project will have three components (Carousel, CarouselButton, and CarouselSlide), it's going to have three test files. Rather than duplicate the Enzyme configuration logic across all three, we should move that logic into a "setup file" that will only run once whenever Jest runs our tests.

Actually, we're going to need two files: the setup file, and a Jest configuration to point to it. Let's start with the configuration. By default, Jest looks for a file called jest.config.js in the root of the project:

ch3/jest.config.js
```
module.exports = {
  setupTestFrameworkScriptFile: './src/tests/jestSetup.js',
};
```

❶ The setupTestFrameworkScriptFile entry tells Jest to go ahead and "Run the file called src/tests/jestSetup.js in the root of this project before running any tests."

Jest supports many other configuration options, but we won't be needing them. If you're curious, consult the official docs.[9]

Now let's create that file:

ch3/src/tests/jestSetup.js
```
import Adapter from 'enzyme-adapter-react-16';
import { configure } from 'enzyme';

configure({ adapter: new Adapter() });
```

If you're running Wallaby or jest --watchAll, you'll need to restart it in order for Jest to recognize the new setup.

> ## Linting and Project Structure
>
> Why put the Jest setup file in the tests directory? Although the Jest setup file isn't a test file, it does run in the same environment as the test files. That means that it should follow the Jest-specific linter rules defined in src/tests/.eslintrc.js. At this point the setup file satisfies either set of linter rules, but that could change if the test setup grows more elaborate.
>
> It's always useful to remember which environment each JavaScript file in your project runs in, and to keep it in a directory with an appropriate ESLint configuration. Ideally, we'd move jest.config.js and wallaby.js into a more precisely configured directory as well, but (as of this writing) Jest and Wallaby expect those files to live in the project root.

---

9. https://jestjs.io/docs/en/configuration.html

With the Jest setup file in place, you no longer need to run Enzyme's configure() method in each individual test file:

```
ch3/src/tests/CarouselButton.test.js
import React from 'react';
import { shallow } from 'enzyme';
import CarouselButton from '../CarouselButton';

describe('CarouselButton', () => {
  const text = 'Button text';
  let wrapper;

  beforeEach(() => {
    wrapper = shallow(<CarouselButton>{text}</CarouselButton>);
  });

  it('renders a <button>', () => {
    expect(wrapper.type()).toBe('button');
  });

  it('passes `children` through to the <button>', () => {
    expect(wrapper.prop('children')).toBe(text);
  });

  it('passes other props through to the <button>', () => {
    const onClick = () => {};
    const className = 'my-carousel-button';
    const dataAction = 'prev';
    wrapper.setProps({ onClick, className, 'data-action': dataAction });
    expect(wrapper.prop('onClick')).toBe(onClick);
    expect(wrapper.prop('className')).toBe(className);
    expect(wrapper.prop('data-action')).toBe(dataAction);
  });
});
```

Commit your improved testing setup:

:wrench: Add Jest setup file

With that in place, it's time to build CarouselButton's sibling, CarouselSlide.

Testing Nested Markup

So far, we've used React to encapsulate the functionality of a single DOM element (<button>) in a component (CarouselButton). But React components are capable of doing more than that. Next, we'll build the CarouselSlide component, which will be responsible for rendering several distinct DOM elements:

- An <img> to display the actual image
- A <figcaption> to associate caption text with the image

- Text, some of which will be wrapped in <strong> for emphasis
- A <figure> to wrap it all up

We'll take a TDD approach to building this tree while ensuring that the props we provide to CarouselSlide are routed correctly. Start by creating a "stub" of the component, a minimal implementation you can add functionality to later:

```
// src/CarouselSlide.js
import React from 'react';

const CarouselSlide = () => <figure />;

export default CarouselSlide;
```

Now for the tests! A good way to start is to check that the right type of DOM element is rendered:

```
// src/tests/CarouselSlide.test.js
import React from 'react';
import { shallow } from 'enzyme';
import CarouselSlide from '../CarouselSlide';

describe('CarouselSlide', () => {
  it('renders a <figure>', () => {
    const wrapper = shallow(<CarouselSlide />);
    expect(wrapper.type()).toBe('figure');
  });
});
```

This test should be green. So let's add some requirements. We want the <figure> to contain two children: an <img> and a <figcaption>, in that order. Enzyme's shallow wrapper API has a childAt(index) method that should be helpful here:

```
// src/tests/CarouselSlide.test.js
...
describe('CarouselSlide', () => {
  let wrapper;

  beforeEach(() => {
    wrapper = shallow(<CarouselSlide />);
  });

  it('renders a <figure>', () => {
    expect(wrapper.type()).toBe('figure');
  });

  it('renders an <img> and a <figcaption> as children', () => {
    expect(wrapper.childAt(0).type()).toBe('img');
    expect(wrapper.childAt(1).type()).toBe('figcaption');
  });
});
...
```

Root and Descendant Wrappers in Enzyme

The object returned by wrapper.childAt(index) is a shallow wrapper, with support for most of the same methods as wrapper itself—but not all. A quirk of Enzyme's API is that wrapper really represents two things: the React tree returned by CarouselSlide's render() function, and the CarouselSlide instance itself. A shallow wrapper around any descendant of the root represents only that node in the tree.

For example, the shallow wrapper at the root of a tree supports both reading props from the root node (wrapper.prop(propName)) and setting props on the component (wrapper.setProps(props)). By contrast, a shallow wrapper around a descendant node supports reading props from that node with node.prop(propName), but the notion of setting props on that node is meaningless. Props in a render tree must come from the component that returned that render tree.

In short: when it comes to testing, components are read/write. Nodes rendered by a component are read-only.

The new test will be red, since <img> and <figcaption> don't yet exist. Add them to the CarouselSlide render tree:

```
// src/CarouselSlide.js
...
const CarouselSlide = () => (
  <figure>
    <img />
    <figcaption />
  </figure>
);
...
```

That should put you in the green. Next, we need to add content. For that, we'll supply three props:

1. imgUrl, a URL for the image displayed in the slide
2. description, a short piece of caption text
3. attribution, the name of image's author

The imgUrl will be used as the src for the <img> tag. Add a test:

```
// src/tests/CarouselSlide.test.js
...
it('passes `imgUrl` through to the <img>', () => {
  const imgUrl = 'https://example.com/image.png';
  wrapper.setProps({ imgUrl });
  const img = wrapper.find('img');
  expect(img.prop('src')).toBe(imgUrl);
});
...
```

❶ Enzyme's find() method takes a CSS-like query selector and returns a shallow wrapper around the result(s).

We could have used childAt(0) again, but using find('img') has the advantage of not breaking if we change our DOM structure, say by reversing the order of <img> and <figcaption>. It makes sense to have one test fail when that happens, but there's no reason to have multiple tests be so rigid. As long as an <img> with the given imgUrl is rendered *somewhere* in the CarouselSlide tree, this test should be happy.

Modify CarouselSlide so that the imgUrl test turns green, then come back to the tests. For description and attribution, we'll want both to be rendered in <figcaption>, with the description bolded by a <strong> tag:

```
// src/tests/CarouselSlide.test.js
...
it('uses `description` and `attribution` as the <figcaption>', () => {
  const description = 'A jaw-droppingly spectacular image';
  const attribution = 'Trevor Burnham';
  wrapper.setProps({ description, attribution });
  expect(wrapper.find('figcaption').text()).toBe(
    `${description} ${attribution}`
  );
  expect(wrapper.find('figcaption strong').text()).toBe(description);
});
...
```

The text() method gives you all rendered text nodes in an element, ignoring any DOM nodes that might be present. The first assertion here looks at all of the text within the <figcaption>; the second looks at the text within the <strong> tag within the <figcaption>.

Try making all tests pass. When you're done, your implementation should look something like this:

```
// src/CarouselSlide.js
...
const CarouselSlide = props => (
  <figure>
    <img src={props.imgUrl} />
    <figcaption>
      <strong>{props.description}</strong> {props.attribution}
    </figcaption>
  </figure>
);
...
```

At this point, ESLint will complain about the missing propTypes for the props used in the render function. Go ahead and add them:

```
// src/CarouselSlide.js
import React from 'react';
➤ import PropTypes from 'prop-types';

  ...

➤ CarouselSlide.propTypes = {
➤   imgUrl: PropTypes.string.isRequired,
➤   description: PropTypes.node.isRequired,
➤   attribution: PropTypes.node,
➤ };

export default CarouselSlide;
```

This change satisfies ESLint, but adds console errors when running Jest:

```
console.error node_modules/prop-types/checkPropTypes.js:19
  Warning: Failed prop type: The prop `imgUrl` is marked as required in
  `CarouselSlide`, but its value is `undefined`.
      in CarouselSlide
console.error node_modules/prop-types/checkPropTypes.js:19
  Warning: Failed prop type: The prop `description` is marked as required in
  `CarouselSlide`, but its value is `undefined`.
      in CarouselSlide
```

To fix this, modify the beforeEach() block so those required props are always set:

```
// src/tests/CarouselSlide.test.js
  ...
  beforeEach(() => {
➤   wrapper = shallow(
➤     <CarouselSlide
➤       imgUrl="https://example.com/default.jpg"
➤       description="Default test image"
➤     />
➤   );
  });
  ...
```

There's one feature still missing from the component: in order to support styling, we should pass the className and style props through to the <figure>. In fact, for maximum flexibility, we should allow event handlers, data-attributes, etc. In short: we should pass every prop *except* the three we're explicitly using through to the <figure>.

Add a test that sets an arbitrary assortment of props as the finishing touch on CarouselSlide.test.js for this chapter:

ch3/src/tests/CarouselSlide.test.js

```javascript
import React from 'react';
import { shallow } from 'enzyme';
import CarouselSlide from '../CarouselSlide';

describe('CarouselSlide', () => {
  let wrapper;

  beforeEach(() => {
    wrapper = shallow(
      <CarouselSlide
        imgUrl="https://example.com/default.jpg"
        description="Default test image"
      />
    );
  });

  it('renders a <figure>', () => {
    expect(wrapper.type()).toBe('figure');
  });

  it('renders an <img> and a <figcaption> as children', () => {
    expect(wrapper.childAt(0).type()).toBe('img');
    expect(wrapper.childAt(1).type()).toBe('figcaption');
  });

  it('passes `imgUrl` through to the <img>', () => {
    const imgUrl = 'https://example.com/image.png';
    wrapper.setProps({ imgUrl });
    const img = wrapper.find('img');
    expect(img.prop('src')).toBe(imgUrl);
  });

  it('uses `description` and `attribution` as the <figcaption>', () => {
    const description = 'A jaw-droppingly spectacular image';
    const attribution = 'Trevor Burnham';
    wrapper.setProps({ description, attribution });
    expect(wrapper.find('figcaption').text()).toBe(
      `${description} ${attribution}`
    );
    expect(wrapper.find('figcaption strong').text()).toBe(description);
  });

  it('passes other props through to the <figure>', () => {
    const style = {};
    const onClick = () => {};
    const className = 'my-carousel-slide';
    wrapper.setProps({ style, onClick, className });
    expect(wrapper.prop('style')).toBe(style);
    expect(wrapper.prop('onClick')).toBe(onClick);
    expect(wrapper.prop('className')).toBe(className);
  });
});
```

The most common way to implement this functionality is with the *object rest syntax.* Here's what it looks like:

```
ch3/src/CarouselSlide.js
import React from 'react';
import PropTypes from 'prop-types';

const CarouselSlide = ({ imgUrl, description, attribution, ...rest }) => (
  <figure {...rest} >
    <img src={imgUrl} />
    <figcaption>
      <strong>{description}</strong> {attribution}
    </figcaption>
  </figure>
);

CarouselSlide.propTypes = {
  imgUrl: PropTypes.string.isRequired,
  description: PropTypes.node.isRequired,
  attribution: PropTypes.node,
};

export default CarouselSlide;
```

❶ As before, the function only takes a single argument, but now that argument is destructured: the values for the object keys imgUrl, description, and attribution are assigned to variables with those same names, and an object consisting of everything else in that object is assigned to a variable called rest using the destructuring spread syntax, ...rest.

❷ Conversely, the JSX spread {...rest} takes the key-value pairs from the rest object and converts them into props. Since rest was originally created from the leftover props given to CarouselSlide, the effect is to pass those props— everything but imgUrl, description, and attribution—through to the <figure>.

You may be familiar with the rest/spread syntax from argument lists and arrays, where it's been supported since ES6. The object rest/spread syntax is newer, and is part of the cutting-edge (as of this writing) ES2018 specification. Happily, this syntax is already included in our project's Babel configuration as part of @babel/preset-react. Sadly, ESLint doesn't want to play along:

```
/Users/tburnham/code/test-driven-carousel/CarouselSlide.js
  4:60  error  Parsing error: Unexpected token ..
```

We've specified ecmaVersion: 6 in our ESLint configuration, and ESLint is holding us to it! The easiest fix would be to specify ecmaVersion: 2018. However, later in this chapter we're going to take advantage of some features that aren't part of any ECMAScript standard yet. To make ESLint understand those syntax features, we need to tell it to use Babel as its parser.

Install a new dev dependency, babel-eslint:[10]

```
$ npm install --save-dev babel-eslint@10.0.1
+ babel-eslint@10.0.1
```

Then replace the entire parserOptions entry in the base ESLint config with a parser entry, giving us our final .eslintrc.js for the chapter:

```
ch3/.eslintrc.js
module.exports = {
  plugins: ['react'],
  extends: ['eslint:recommended', 'plugin:react/recommended'],
  parser: 'babel-eslint',
  env: {
    node: true,
  },
  rules: {
    quotes: ['error', 'single', { avoidEscape: true }],
    'comma-dangle': ['error', 'always-multiline'],
  },
  settings: {
    react: {
      version: '16.4.2',
    },
  },
};
```

Problem solved! With babel-eslint as its parser, ESLint understands all of the syntactic features we're relying on Babel for.

CarouselSlide and its tests should be looking ship-shape now. Make a commit:

```
:sparkles: Initial implementation of CarouselSlide
```

Just one component to go: Carousel itself.

Testing Stateful Components

Both of the React components we've built so far are *stateless*: their render output is determined entirely by the props they receive, allowing us to express them as a single function. This has the advantage of simplicity. But a carousel is *stateful*: it needs to keep track of which slide it's currently showing. In this section, we'll take a TDD approach to building a Carousel component with internal state.

Start with a stub implementation of the component. Since functional components can't have state, make it a subclass of React.PureComponent:

---

10. https://github.com/babel/babel-eslint

```
// src/Carousel.js
import React from 'react';

class Carousel extends React.PureComponent {
  render() {
    return <div />;
  }
}

export default Carousel;
```

Using React.PureComponent instead of React.Component tells React that our component doesn't need to be re-rendered unless its props or state change. It's a good practice to keep components pure whenever possible, both for performance and for conceptual simplicity.

Add a skeletal test suite:

```
// src/tests/Carousel.test.js
import React from 'react';
import { shallow } from 'enzyme';
import Carousel from '../Carousel';
describe('Carousel', () => {
  let wrapper;

  beforeEach(() => {
    wrapper = shallow(<Carousel />);
  });

  it('renders a <div>', () => {
    expect(wrapper.type()).toBe('div');
  });
});
```

Now let's outline some requirements for this component:

- The carousel keeps track of the current slide with a number, slideIndex.

- slideIndex is initially 0, meaning that the first slide is shown.

- Clicking the "Prev" button decreases slideIndex, wrapping around to the index of the last slide when it would go below 0.

- Clicking the "Next" button increases slideIndex, wrapping around to 0 when it would go above the index of the last slide.

- The carousel takes an array named slides and renders the slide indicated by slideIndex.

Translating these requirements into tests will help us figure out exactly how to implement them.

Testing State

Enzyme's API for working with state is analogous to its API for working with props. Call wrapper.state(key) to get the piece of state corresponding to that key:

```
// src/tests/Carousel.test.js
...
it('has an initial `slideIndex` of 0', () => {
  expect(wrapper.state('slideIndex')).toBe(0);
});
...
```

To satisfy this test, you need Carousel to attach a state object to itself when it's instantiated. One way to do that would be to add a constructor(). However, you can do better using the "class properties" syntax, which let you define instance properties as if they were variables scoped inside of a class block:

```
// src/Carousel.js
...
class Carousel extends React.PureComponent {
  state = {
    slideIndex: 0,
  };

  render() {
    return <div />;
  }
}
...
```

This syntax isn't supported out-of-the-box by @babel/preset-react or @babel/preset-env, but it's become enormously popular in the React community. To add it to the project, install the @babel/plugin-proposal-class-properties plugin:

```
$ npm install --save-dev @babel/plugin-proposal-class-properties@7.1.0
+ @babel/plugin-proposal-class-properties@7.1.0
```

That addition yields the final package.json for the chapter:

```
ch3/package.json
{
  "name": "test-driven-carousel",
  "version": "1.0.0",
  "description": "",
  "main": "index.js",
  "scripts": {
    "test": "jest",
    "lint": "eslint . && prettier-eslint --list-different **/*.js",
    "format": "prettier-eslint --write **/*.js"
  },
```

```
    "keywords": [],
    "author": "",
    "license": "ISC",
    "devDependencies": {
      "@babel/core": "^7.2.0",
      "@babel/plugin-proposal-class-properties": "^7.1.0",
      "@babel/preset-env": "^7.2.0",
      "@babel/preset-react": "^7.0.0",
      "babel-core": "^7.0.0-bridge.0",
      "babel-eslint": "^10.0.1",
      "babel-jest": "^23.6.0",
      "enzyme": "^3.8.0",
      "enzyme-adapter-react-16": "^1.7.1",
      "eslint": "^5.10.0",
      "eslint-plugin-jest": "^22.1.2",
      "eslint-plugin-react": "^7.11.1",
      "jest": "^23.6.0",
      "prettier-eslint-cli": "^4.7.1",
      "react-dom": "^16.4.2"
    },
    "dependencies": {
      "prop-types": "^15.7.2",
      "react": "^16.4.2"
    }
  }
```

Now add a plugins entry to .babelrc.js. Plugins listed there are combined with those provided by the presets:

```
ch3/.babelrc.js
module.exports = {
  presets: ['@babel/preset-react', '@babel/preset-env'],
➤ plugins: ['@babel/plugin-proposal-class-properties'],
};
```

With this added Babel plugin, Carousel's initial state should work as intended. Now to make the component interactive!

Testing Event Handlers

To give the user a way to change the slideIndex, the Carousel component needs some buttons:

```
// src/tests/Carousel.test.js
...
➤ import CarouselButton from '../CarouselButton';

describe('Carousel', () => {
➤   ...
➤   it('renders a CarouselButton labeled "Prev"', () => {
➤     expect(
```

```
      wrapper
        .find(CarouselButton)
        .at(0)
        .prop('children')
    ).toBe('Prev');
  });

  it('renders a CarouselButton labeled "Next"', () => {
    expect(
      wrapper
        .find(CarouselButton)
        .at(1)
        .prop('children')
    ).toBe('Next');
  });
});
```

❶ find() uses the CarouselButton component itself as a selector. The string 'CarouselButton' would also work here, but string selectors are less reliable, since they depend on a detail of the target component (displayName) that's otherwise hidden from you.

❷ Since find() returns multiple results, at(index) is used to get a shallow wrapper around an individual button.

❸ prop('children') returns what was passed as the children prop to the CarouselButton. Note that text() only works for DOM elements, not for components.

Jump to the implementation and add the buttons to the render tree:

```
// src/Carousel.js
import React from 'react';
import CarouselButton from './CarouselButton';

class Carousel extends React.PureComponent {
  ...
  render() {
    return (
      <div>
        <CarouselButton>Prev</CarouselButton>
        <CarouselButton>Next</CarouselButton>
      </div>
    );
  }
}
...
```

Now we need to simulate click events on the "Prev" and "Next" buttons. Rather than relying on the relative order of the buttons in the render tree for every test, add data- attributes to make our test selectors more self-explanatory. The names of the attributes will have no effect on the functionality of the app. So, render the "Prev" button with data-action="prev" and the "Next" button with data-action="next", making it a breeze to target them with find(selector):

```
// src/tests/Carousel.test.js
...
➤ it('decrements `slideIndex` when Prev is clicked', () => {
➤   wrapper.setState({ slideIndex: 1 });
➤   wrapper.find('[data-action="prev"]').simulate('click');
➤   expect(wrapper.state('slideIndex')).toBe(0);
➤ });
➤
➤ it('increments `slideIndex` when Next is clicked', () => {
➤   wrapper.setState({ slideIndex: 1 });
➤   wrapper.find('[data-action="next"]').simulate('click');
➤   expect(wrapper.state('slideIndex')).toBe(2);
➤ });
    ...
```

The simulate('click') calls trigger the onClick handler attached to the target node.

Now add the data- attrs (as props) to the buttons, along with click handlers:

```
// src/Carousel.js
    ...
❶ handlePrevClick = () => {
❷   this.setState(({ slideIndex }) => ({ slideIndex: slideIndex - 1 }));
➤ };
➤
➤ handleNextClick = () => {
➤   this.setState(({ slideIndex }) => ({ slideIndex: slideIndex + 1 }));
➤ };
    render() {
      return (
➤       <div>
➤         <CarouselButton data-action="prev" onClick={this.handlePrevClick}>
➤           Prev
➤         </CarouselButton>
➤         <CarouselButton data-action="next" onClick={this.handleNextClick}>
➤           Next
➤         </CarouselButton>
➤       </div>
      );
    }
    ...
```

❶ The click handlers are defined using the same class property syntax used for state, which automatically binds them to the component instance. To put a finer point on it: new copies of state, handlePrevClick(), and handleNextClick() are created for every instance of Carousel.

❷ Previously, we've used setState() with a state update object as its argument. Here, it's given a callback instead. The callback receives the original state and returns an update object. This is a helpful approach for avoiding timing issues: setState() is asynchronous, so it's possible in principle for multiple state changes to be queued up. If, for instance, a "Prev" click and a "Next" click both registered before the state changes flushed (unlikely but theoretically possible), the correct result would be for the two slideIndex changes to cancel each other out, which is exactly what the two callbacks would do.

With that, the tests should be green. Sharp-eyed readers will notice that the click handlers don't yet handle the case where slideIndex would go too low or too high and need to wrap around. In order to do that, Carousel needs to know how many slides there are. Which brings us to our final Carousel feature: rendering the slides.

Manipulating State in Tests

So far, the carousel is just a pair of buttons. What it really needs is some slides. A simple approach to this is to give the Carousel instance an array of data as a prop called slides, then pass the data from slides[slideIndex] as props to a CarouselSlide.

Replace the existing beforeEach block to set the slides prop on the Carousel instance, then add a (failing) test for the slide-passing behavior:

```
// src/tests/Carousel.test.js
import React from 'react';
import { shallow } from 'enzyme';
import Carousel from '../Carousel';
import CarouselButton from '../CarouselButton';
import CarouselSlide from '../CarouselSlide';

describe('Carousel', () => {
  let wrapper;

  const slides = [
    {
      imgUrl: 'https://example.com/slide1.png',
      description: 'Slide 1',
      attribution: 'Uno Pizzeria',
    },
    {
      imgUrl: 'https://example.com/slide2.png',
      description: 'Slide 2',
      attribution: 'Dos Equis',
    },
```

```
    {
      imgUrl: 'https://example.com/slide3.png',
      description: 'Slide 3',
      attribution: 'Three Amigos',
    },
  ];

  beforeEach(() => {
    wrapper = shallow(<Carousel slides={slides} />);
  });

  ...

  it('renders the current slide as a CarouselSlide', () => {
    let slideProps;
    slideProps = wrapper.find(CarouselSlide).props();
    expect(slideProps).toEqual(slides[0]);
    wrapper.setState({ slideIndex: 1 });
    slideProps = wrapper.find(CarouselSlide).props();
    expect(slideProps).toEqual(slides[1]);
  });
});
```

❶ The new test uses a method called props() instead of prop(). This method returns an object containing all of the node's props.

❷ Recall that toEqual() does a deep comparison of two objects, whereas toBe() does a strict equality check. Strict equality would fail here; there's no way to replace all of a component instance's props with a different object, even if we wanted to. Instead, what we're checking is: "Does this component have all of the props from slides[0], and no other props?"

❸ Enzyme's setState() method works analogously to setProps(), merging the given object into the component's existing state.

Then update the render method in Carousel to satisfy the test:

```
// src/Carousel.js
import React from 'react';
import CarouselButton from './CarouselButton';
import CarouselSlide from './CarouselSlide';

class Carousel extends React.PureComponent {
  state = {
    slideIndex: 0,
  };

  handlePrevClick = () => {
    this.setState(({ slideIndex }) => ({ slideIndex: slideIndex - 1 }));
  };
```

```
    handleNextClick = () => {
      this.setState(({ slideIndex }) => ({ slideIndex: slideIndex + 1 }));
    };

    render() {
      const { slides, ...rest } = this.props;
      return (
        <div {...rest}>
          <CarouselSlide {...slides[this.state.slideIndex]} />
          <CarouselButton data-action="prev" onClick={this.handlePrevClick}>
            Prev
          </CarouselButton>
          <CarouselButton data-action="next" onClick={this.handleNextClick}>
            Next
          </CarouselButton>
        </div>
      );
    }
  }

  export default Carousel;
```

❶ The ...slides[this.state.slideIndex] spread passes every key-value pair in the object into the <CarouselSlide>, satisfying our test.

Having slides as an array also allows us to solve the slideIndex "overflow" problem: in the Next click handler, you can use slides.length as an upper bound and wrap to 0 when the new index would collide with that bound. Conversely, in the Prev click handler, you can wrap from 0 to the max value of slides.length - 1. Write some tests to make this concrete:

ch3/src/tests/Carousel.test.js

```
import React from 'react';
import { shallow } from 'enzyme';
import Carousel from '../Carousel';
import CarouselButton from '../CarouselButton';
import CarouselSlide from '../CarouselSlide';

describe('Carousel', () => {
  let wrapper;

  const slides = [
    {
      imgUrl: 'https://example.com/slide1.png',
      description: 'Slide 1',
      attribution: 'Uno Pizzeria',
    },
    {
      imgUrl: 'https://example.com/slide2.png',
      description: 'Slide 2',
      attribution: 'Dos Equis',
    },
```

```
    {
      imgUrl: 'https://example.com/slide3.png',
      description: 'Slide 3',
      attribution: 'Three Amigos',
    },
  ];

  beforeEach(() => {
    wrapper = shallow(<Carousel slides={slides} />);
  });

  it('renders a <div>', () => {
    expect(wrapper.type()).toBe('div');
  });

  it('has an initial `slideIndex` of 0', () => {
    expect(wrapper.state('slideIndex')).toBe(0);
  });

  it('renders a CarouselButton labeled "Prev"', () => {
    expect(
      wrapper
        .find(CarouselButton)
        .at(0)
        .prop('children')
    ).toBe('Prev');
  });

  it('renders a CarouselButton labeled "Next"', () => {
    expect(
      wrapper
        .find(CarouselButton)
        .at(1)
        .prop('children')
    ).toBe('Next');
  });
  describe('with a middle slide selected', () => {
    beforeEach(() => {
      wrapper.setState({ slideIndex: 1 });
    });

    it('decrements `slideIndex` when Prev is clicked', () => {
      wrapper.find('[data-action="prev"]').simulate('click');
      expect(wrapper.state('slideIndex')).toBe(0);
    });

    it('increments `slideIndex` when Next is clicked', () => {
      wrapper.setState({ slideIndex: 1 });
      wrapper.find('[data-action="next"]').simulate('click');
      expect(wrapper.state('slideIndex')).toBe(2);
    });
  });
```

❶

```
describe('with the first slide selected', () => {
  it('wraps `slideIndex` to the max value when Prev is clicked', () => {
    wrapper.setState({ slideIndex: 0 });
    wrapper.find('[data-action="prev"]').simulate('click');
    expect(wrapper.state('slideIndex')).toBe(slides.length - 1);
  });
});

describe('with the last slide selected', () => {
  it('wraps `slideIndex` to the min value when Next is clicked', () => {
    wrapper.setState({ slideIndex: slides.length - 1 });
    wrapper.find('[data-action="next"]').simulate('click');
    expect(wrapper.state('slideIndex')).toBe(0);
  });
});

it('renders the current slide as a CarouselSlide', () => {
  let slideProps;
  slideProps = wrapper.find(CarouselSlide).props();
  expect(slideProps).toEqual(slides[0]);
  wrapper.setState({ slideIndex: 1 });
  slideProps = wrapper.find(CarouselSlide).props();
  expect(slideProps).toEqual(slides[1]);
});
});
```

❶ The original click handler tests are now in a describe() block to make their initial condition explicit, and two new describe() blocks have been added below it for the edge cases.

Now all you have to do is update the handlers:

```
// src/Carousel.js
...
handlePrevClick = () => {
  const { slides } = this.props;
  this.setState(({ slideIndex }) => ({
    slideIndex: (slideIndex + slides.length - 1) % slides.length,
  }));
};

handleNextClick = () => {
  const { slides } = this.props;
  this.setState(({ slideIndex }) => ({
    slideIndex: (slideIndex + 1) % slides.length,
  }));
};
...
```

❶ The remainder operator (%) makes it possible to deal with the click handler edge cases succinctly.

One last thing: you'll need to declare propTypes in order to make the linter happy. This time, use the static keyword to declare them as a static property within the class definition:

ch3/src/Carousel.js
```
import React from 'react';
import PropTypes from 'prop-types';
import CarouselButton from './CarouselButton';
import CarouselSlide from './CarouselSlide';

class Carousel extends React.PureComponent {
  static propTypes = {
    slides: PropTypes.arrayOf(PropTypes.shape(CarouselSlide.propTypes))
      .isRequired,
  };

  state = {
    slideIndex: 0,
  };

  handlePrevClick = () => {
    const { slides } = this.props;
    this.setState(({ slideIndex }) => ({
      slideIndex: (slideIndex + slides.length - 1) % slides.length,
    }));
  };

  handleNextClick = () => {
    const { slides } = this.props;
    this.setState(({ slideIndex }) => ({
      slideIndex: (slideIndex + 1) % slides.length,
    }));
  };

  render() {
    const { slides, ...rest } = this.props;
    return (
      <div {...rest}>
        <CarouselSlide {...slides[this.state.slideIndex]} />
        <CarouselButton data-action="prev" onClick={this.handlePrevClick}>
          Prev
        </CarouselButton>
        <CarouselButton data-action="next" onClick={this.handleNextClick}>
          Next
        </CarouselButton>
      </div>
    );
  }
}

export default Carousel;
```

These prop types say, "slides must be an array of objects that each have the same shape as the propTypes declared by CarouselSlide."

With that, this chapter's Carousel is complete! Put a bow on it with a commit:

```
:sparkles: Initial implementation of Carousel component
```

Mantra: Test One Piece at a Time

There are two schools of thought on unit testing. One is that the tests should be as realistic as possible. In this view, tests against one component should depend on the behavior not only of that one component, but also of its dependencies. The other school of thought, the one applied in this book, is that tests should describe the behavior of their target in isolation, not the behavior within a complete system. To test the complete system, you must test each part on its own. This requires diligence and thoroughness, but the reward is that changes to a single component can only fail that component's tests, rather than a perplexing cascade of failures. That's why this chapter's mantra is: *"Test one piece at a time."*

You've seen how testing in isolation can be achieved in React using Enzyme's shallow() method: changes to any one of the three components you created can only fail the tests for that particular component. Conversely, writing a test doesn't require you to think about the behavior of anything but the component being tested. Look at the component and its tests side-by-side, and you can see a direct correspondence. This is the cardinal advantage of shallow testing over testing against the complete DOM tree generated by the component, the approach favored by react-testing-library.

Now to recap. In this chapter, you learned how Babel makes it possible to write React code with the succinct JSX syntax. You set up ESLint to preemptively warn you about common React mistakes. Finally, you built a React carousel the TDD way, writing tests with Jest and Enzyme for each piece of functionality you added. In the next chapter, you'll add a much-needed coat of paint with styled-components, a unit-testable alternative to conventional stylesheets. And you'll use webpack to build your project for the browser so that you can see your carousel in action.

CHAPTER 4

Styling in JavaScript with Styled-Components

Take a moment to consider the unlikely origins of the web as an app platform. When Tim Berners-Lee wrote the original web server and browser in 1990, web pages were written in a single language: HTML. HTML could only convey raw content; the way that content was presented was left to the browser. Gradually, a handful of stylistic choices were added to the markup language. Authors started to embellish their sites with (often garish) color and font choices, not to mention the infamous <marquee> tag. With the introduction of CSS in 1996, the aesthetic choices available to web designers exploded.

Around the same time that CSS was making headway, JavaScript began to bring interactivity to the web. The introduction of Gmail in 2004 proved that it was possible to build web apps that could rival their desktop counterparts, and with obvious advantages: no installation, instant updates, and access from any web-capable device. Developers flocked to the new platform. Since then, the three languages of the web—HTML, CSS, and JavaScript—have co-evolved, adding features to better complement each other. Miraculously, that evolution has allowed the web to compete with native app platforms even though none of its languages were invented with apps in mind.

Fast-forward to today. React has transformed web development by allowing developers to express the page's markup as a function of application state. But CSS remains largely static. In React apps that follow the tradition of keeping JavaScript and CSS separate, a layer of indirection is required in order to apply CSS rules based on application state: developers must write React components that render elements with particular class names based on their state, then write CSS rules for those class names to express the desired styles. As the list of CSS rules grow, developers inevitably struggle to keep them organized. The situation gets worse when components want to override the styles of other components they render, as "specificity wars" break out between the competing CSS rules.

Happily, there's a solution for many of these problems: *CSS-in-JS*, a paradigm exemplified by the popular styled-components library. With CSS-in-JS, you write styles using the familiar CSS syntax, but the actual style rules are generated at runtime as needed. This has enormous advantages for code organization and maintainability. And, not incidentally for the topic of this book, it also allows style rules to be subjected to unit tests.

In this chapter, you'll add styling to our carousel components from the previous chapter using styled-components. You'll make assertions about the components' styles using Enzyme, and capture them with Jest's snapshots feature. But before you start styling, let's take a brief digression into webpack, a tool that bridges the gap between your components and the browser.

Packaging an App with webpack

In the beginning, preparing JavaScript for the browser was simple: put your page's functionality in a single script and loaded it with a <script> tag. Then jQuery took off, and your script had a dependency. No problem: jQuery + app = two <script> tags. But then other libraries came around, which depended in turn on other libraries. Using Backbone.js? Better load it after Underscore.js. As more app functionality moved into the browser, the once simple act of loading code in the right order became a challenge. And what about concatenating and minifying scripts for performance? What about loading "below-the-fold" scripts asynchronously? What about development mode?

Only a few years ago, bespoke in-house tools were the norm for addressing these problems. But now, at last, there's a Swiss Army knife for building JavaScript: webpack[1] (always lowercase). Raw scripts go into webpack; compiled, concatenated, minified bundles come out. With a little bit of configuration (OK, sometimes a lot), webpack can generate any bundle you can imagine.

In this section, you're going to harness the power of webpack to build a small demo app for the carousel component. To get started, open the test-driven-carousel project from the last chapter. Then install webpack as a dev dependency, along with webpack-cli and a library called babel-loader that lets webpack use Babel to compile scripts:

---

1.   https://webpack.js.org/

```
$ npm install --save-dev webpack@4.26.1 webpack-cli@3.1.2 babel-loader@8.0.4
+ webpack@4.26.1
+ webpack-cli@3.1.2
+ babel-loader@8.0.4
```

Then create a file called webpack.config.js in the root of the project:

```
// webpack.config.js
module.exports = {
  mode: 'development',
  entry: {
    carousel: './src/Carousel.js',
  },
  module: {
    rules: [
      {
        test: /\.js$/,
        loader: require.resolve('babel-loader'),
      },
    ],
  },
};
```

❶ Using mode: 'development' provides good defaults for running code locally, optimizing for ease of debugging at the expense of bundle size and runtime performance. By contrast, mode: 'production' would give you a minified bundle.

❷ Each entry point defines a separate bundle for webpack to build. Here we're telling webpack to build a bundle called carousel.js that contains src/Carousel.js and its dependencies.

❸ The module block is where we tell webpack how to treat different kinds of modules, via an array of rules. A "module" in webpack can be any kind of file—JSON, CSS, even images—but we're only concerned with JS modules, so we have just one rule.

❹ This rule says "Use babel-loader for all .js files." The loader will run each script through Babel with the config found in the root of our project.

The webpack-cli package added an executable named webpack. When it runs, it looks for a config file to tell it what to do. Although it should find the webpack.config.js in the root of the project by default, make the connection explicit by passing it a --config flag in a new build script:

```
// package.json
...
"scripts": {
  "test": "jest",
  "lint": "eslint . && prettier-eslint --list-different **/*.js",
  "format": "prettier-eslint --write **/*.js",
  "build": "webpack --config webpack.config.js"
},
...
```

Now try building your project:

```
$ npm run build
Hash: ccc06a7f00b25a1780c4
Version: webpack 4.26.1
Time: 619ms
Built at: 2018-12-02 18:48:29
        Asset     Size     Chunks          Chunk Names
carousel.js  106 KiB  carousel  [emitted]  carousel
Entrypoint carousel = carousel.js
[./src/Carousel.js] 5.31 KiB {carousel} [built]
[./src/CarouselButton.js] 269 bytes {carousel} [built]
[./src/CarouselSlide.js] 1.46 KiB {carousel} [built]
    + 11 hidden modules
```

If you look in the dist dir of the project, you'll see the carousel.js bundle. As the output indicates, that bundle includes Carousel, CarouselButton, and CarouselSlide.

Sharp-eyed readers will notice that the size of the bundle (106 KiB) is many times greater than the total size of the three carousel components. The gap is explained by the "hidden modules" mentioned at the end of the output. By default, webpack is silent regarding modules from node_modules. In this case, those modules are the imports from the react and prop-types packages. If you're curious to see them, run webpack again with the --display-modules flag.

A bit of housekeeping before we continue. ESLint is unaware that dist/carousel.js is generated code, so it considers that code to be within its purview:

```
$ npx eslint .

/Users/tburnham/code/test-driven-carousel/dist/carousel.js
   16:24  error  Missing trailing comma        comma-dangle
   45:48  error  'Symbol' is not defined        no-undef
   ...

✖ 81 problems (81 errors, 0 warnings)
  36 errors and 0 warnings potentially fixable with the `--fix` option.
```

81 errors! Fortunately, ESLint allows you to ignore directories the same way that Git does, by listing patterns in an ignore file:

```
ch4/.eslintignore
dist/
```

It's also a good idea to tell Prettier to ignore that directory:

```
ch4/.prettierignore
dist/
```

Additionally, if you're using VS Code, you might consider adding dist to the
files.exclude section of your Workspace Settings, since you shouldn't have to
view or edit its contents directly:

```
ch4/.vscode/settings.json
{
  "files.exclude": {
    "dist": true,
    "node_modules": true,
    "package-lock.json": true
  },
  "[javascript]": {
    "editor.tabSize": 2
  },
  "editor.formatOnSave": true
}
```

Now you've got a browser-friendly bundle of this project's components! All
you need is an example page to show them off on. But first, save your progress:

```
:wrench: Initial webpack setup
```

Adding an Example Page

Create an example dir. Since it's going to contain web app code, it should be
based on the same ESLint config as the src dir. However, one adjustment is
in order: as it is, the linter will complain any time we return JSX from a
function if that function doesn't declare its arguments as propTypes. This is a
bit of a nuisance, so disable the react/prop-types rule[2] within the example dir:

```
ch4/example/.eslintrc.js
module.exports = {
  env: {
    browser: true,
  },
  rules: {
    "react/prop-types": "off",
  }
};
```

---

2.   https://github.com/yannickcr/eslint-plugin-react/blob/master/docs/rules/prop-types.md

Then add an index.js with some placeholder code:

```
// example/index.js
import React from 'react';
import ReactDOM from 'react-dom';

const container = document.createElement('div');
document.body.appendChild(container);
ReactDOM.render(<h1>Hello, webpack!</h1>, container);
```

Declare that JS file as a second entry point in the project's webpack config:

```
// webpack.config.js
module.exports = {
  mode: 'development',
  entry: {
    carousel: './src/Carousel.js',
➤   example: './example/index.js',
  },
  ...
};
```

We need a page to host this app. Rather than writing up the HTML, you can make webpack generate it as part of the build process using html-webpack-plugin:

```
$ npm install --save-dev html-webpack-plugin@3.2.0
+ html-webpack-plugin@3.2.0
```

Once the plugin is installed, add it to the webpack config:

```
ch4/webpack.config.js
➤ const HtmlWebpackPlugin = require('html-webpack-plugin');
module.exports = {
  mode: 'development',
  entry: {
    carousel: './src/Carousel.js',
    example: './example/index.js',
  },
➤ plugins: [
➤   new HtmlWebpackPlugin({
❶     title: 'Carousel Example',
❷     chunks: ['example'],
➤   }),
➤ ],
  module: {
    rules: [
      {
        test: /\.js$/,
        loader: require.resolve('babel-loader'), },
    ],
  },
};
```

❶ The title option sets the title of the generated HTML page.

❷ By default, the page generated by the plugin includes every bundle listed in entry. We only want the bundle corresponding to the example entrypoint. Later in this chapter, when example/index.js imports the Carousel component, Carousel and all of its dependencies—including React—will be included in the example bundle.

Run another build:

```
$ npm run build
```

Once that completes, you'll see that a dist/index.html has been generated along with the JavaScript assets. Open it up in a browser, and you should see a page with the message rendered by the example code:

> Hello, webpack!

Now you can implement a working carousel example. The bulk of the code is going to be the slides themselves, so create a separate slides.js for that:

```
ch4/example/slides.js
import React from 'react';

const referralParams = 'utm_source=test-driven-carousel&utm_medium=referral';

const getUsernameUrl = username =>
  `https://unsplash.com/@${username}?${referralParams}`;

const getAttribution = ({ name, username }) => (
  <>
    Photo by <a href={getUsernameUrl(username)}>{name}</a> on{' '}
    <a href={`https://unsplash.com/?${referralParams}`}>Unsplash</a>
  </>
);
export default [
  {
    description: 'Seattle',
    attribution: getAttribution({
      name: 'Ganapathy Kumar',
      username: 'gkumar2175',
    }),
    imgUrl:
      'https://images.unsplash.com/photo-1469321461812-afeb94496b27?w=1080' +
      '&ixid=eyJhcHBfaWQiOjIzODE4fQ&s=568095e79ee2cb55a795ad454ac9cf5e',
  },
  {
    description: 'Chicago',
    attribution: getAttribution({
      name: 'Austin Neill',
      username: 'arstyy',
    }),
```

❶

```
      imgUrl:
        'https://images.unsplash.com/photo-1484249170766-998fa6efe3c0?w=1080' +
        '&ixid=eyJhcHBfaWQiOjIzODE4fQ&s=f56c763ccf86e87644b049c9abbcf455',
  },
  {
    description: 'Barcelona',
    attribution: getAttribution({
      name: 'Enes',
      username: 'royalfound',
    }),
    imgUrl:
      'https://images.unsplash.com/photo-1464790719320-516ecd75af6c?w=1080' +
      '&ixid=eyJhcHBfaWQiOjIzODE4fQ&s=e836c604036680eeba5c77ebdb171c73',
  },
  {
    description: 'New York',
    attribution: getAttribution({
      name: 'Anthony DELANOIX',
      username: 'anthonydelanoix',
    }),
    imgUrl:
      'https://images.unsplash.com/photo-1423655156442-ccc11daa4e99?w=1080' +
      '&ixid=eyJhcHBfaWQiOjIzODE4fQ&s=54a272d03f5c06c416e8899f113dff06',
  },
  {
    description: 'Rio de Janeiro',
    attribution: getAttribution({
      name: 'Agustín Diaz',
      username: 'agussdiaz28',
    }),
    imgUrl:
      'https://images.unsplash.com/photo-1483729558449-99ef09a8c325?w=1080' +
      '&ixid=eyJhcHBfaWQiOjIzODE4fQ&s=966003791f746c210b73863cf6170e6c',
  },
];
```

❶ The <> tag is a *fragment*, a special kind of React element that has no corresponding DOM element. Fragments are a relatively new feature, introduced in React 16.2.0.[3]

Then update index.js to render a Carousel with these slides:

```
ch4/example/index.js
import React from 'react';
import ReactDOM from 'react-dom';
➤ import Carousel from '../src/Carousel';
➤ import slides from './slides';
```

---

3. https://reactjs.org/blog/2017/11/28/react-v16.2.0-fragment-support.html

```
const container = document.createElement('div');
document.body.appendChild(container);
➤ ReactDOM.render(<Carousel slides={slides} />, container);
```

> ## Using Unsplash Images
>
> The images used in this book come from Unsplash,[a] a terrific resource for free photos. Please respect their guidelines.[b] Always accompany the photos with proper attribution, as the example application in this book does. If you want to use the photos in a different application, don't copy the URLs from this book. Instead, use the Unsplash API[c] to generate your own.
>
> _____
>
> a. https://unsplash.com/
> b. https://medium.com/unsplash/unsplash-api-guidelines-28e0216e6daa
> c. https://unsplash.com/developers

With that, the example should be ready to view in the browser. Update the JavaScript bundle with npm run build, then refresh the page:

Seattle Photo by Ganapathy Kumar on Unsplash

Prev   Next

Success! That's your carousel component, unstyled but fully functional. This is a good time for a commit using the gitmoji for adding code documentation (there's one for everything!):

```
:bulb: Add example page
```

One last bit of setup before we move on to styled-components. Right now, if you wanted to make changes to either the Carousel components or the example code and see them in the browser, you'd need to run npm run build and refresh the page. Let's improve on that experience.

Running webpack-dev-server

The experience of building an app and the experience of doing local development are closely linked: every time you make changes during local development, you need to run a build. Ideally, those builds should be incremental, meaning that only the code that's changed is recompiled, allowing you to see the new code in the browser as quickly as possible.

Enter webpack-dev-server, the missing link between your local code and your browser. Add it to the project's devDependencies:

```
$ npm install --save-dev webpack-dev-server@3.1.10
+ webpack-dev-server@3.1.10
```

By default, webpack-dev-server serves dist/index.html. That's exactly what we want, so no additional configuration is required. All you need is another scripts entry:

```
// package.json
...
"scripts": {
  "test": "jest",
  "lint": "eslint . && prettier-eslint --list-different **/*.js",
  "format": "prettier-eslint --write **/*.js",
  "build": "webpack --config webpack.config.js",
  "dev": "webpack-dev-server --config webpack.config.js --open"
},
...
```

The --open flag means that webpack-dev-server will open your system's default browser automatically when it's ready. Give it a try:

```
$ npm run dev
> test-driven-carousel@1.0.0 dev /Users/tburnham/code/test-driven-carousel
> webpack-dev-server --open

i ﹁wds﹂: Project is running at http://localhost:8080/
```

And with that, the example app should be open in a new browser tab. Now for the cool part: try making a change to the app. Hit save, and you'll see that change in the browser! What sorcery is this? The dev server injected some code into the browser that listens (via a WebSocket) to the server process. When the server tells it that a change has occurred, the browser code triggers a refresh to bring in the changes.

Hot Module Reloading

Wouldn't it be cool if, instead of the browser refreshing every time you change some code, it could just bring in the new code? Such a thing exists: it's called hot module reloading (HMR), and webpack-dev-server supports it.

However, HMR requires some additional setup, not only on the server side but also in the browser to update the React tree when a component's code changes. These details are outside the scope of this book, but if you're curious, check out the docs for react-hot-loader.[a]

HMR works out of the box when you use Storybook, the documentation tool introduced in Adding Docs with Storybook, on page 154.

---

a.   https://gaearon.github.io/react-hot-loader/

Now that your dev server is fired up, you're ready to start styling. Don't forget to make a commit:

```
:wrench: Initial webpack-dev-server setup
```

Getting Started with Styled-Components

As apps grow, they can contain thousands of style rules—too many for a single person to keep track of. This leads to unintended conflicts. For example, which of the styles below will apply to a disabled button with the white class?

```
// StylesheetA.css
button.white {
  background-color: white;
  color: black;
}

// StylesheetB.css
button:disabled {
  background-color: grey;
  color: darkgrey;
}
```

The answer is that it depends on the order the stylesheets are loaded in, as both selectors have the same level of specificity. This is a very fragile state of affairs for a complex app. Worse, removing style rules becomes a risky endeavor. Let's say that your app has this style rule:

```
p.alert-message {
  color: red;
}
```

You search your codebase for alert-message, find no results, and so you remove the style. But your search didn't match this React code:

```
<p className={`${urgency}-message`}>This is an alert!</p>
```

The CSS-in-JS paradigm, exemplified by styled-components,[4] greatly alleviates these problems by allowing a component's style rules to be written as a function of its props. This offers a number of advantages:

- No need to search your codebase to find out which styles are associated with a component. Its styles are either in the same module, or imported like any other dependency.

- Styles are generated as a function of their component's props and state, just like markup.

- Styles can be subjected to unit tests.

And unlike the style prop, style rules generated by styled-components have the full range of functionality of ordinary CSS, including support for media queries, keyframe animations, and pseudo-classes.

Let's start adding some style to test-driven-carousel. Install the styled-components package as a dependency:

```
$ npm install --save styled-components@4.1.1
+ styled-components@4.1.1
```

So far, this book's modus operandi has been to present tests first, then the code to satisfy these tests. This is, after all, a book about TDD, and TDD is usually taken to mean "writing tests first." But on a deeper level, TDD is about seeking useful feedback for your code as quickly as possible. Tests are just one possible source of feedback. And when it comes to styles, the most useful source of feedback is usually *seeing* those styles.

So set tests aside for now. All you'll need for this section is a live dev server.

Creating a Styled Component

Currently, the <img> created by CarouselSlide is unstyled, which means that it scales to whatever the original size of the image is. That means that the carousel jarringly expands and contracts as users move from slide to slide. Worse, it'll push other page content around in the process. Clearly, this needs to be fixed!

---

4.   https://www.styled-components.com/

To do that, we'll replace the unstyled <img> element with a component generated by styled-components:

```
// src/CarouselSlide.js
import React from 'react';
import PropTypes from 'prop-types';
import styled from 'styled-components';

const Img = styled.img`
  object-fit: cover;
  width: 100%;
  height: 500px;
`;

const CarouselSlide = ({ imgUrl, description, attribution, ...rest }) => (
  <figure {...rest}>
    <Img src={imgUrl} />
    <figcaption>
      <strong>{description}</strong> {attribution}
    </figcaption>
  </figure>
);
...
```

styled.img is a function that generates a component that renders an <img> tag with the given styles. When an instance of that Img component is mounted, styled-components will dynamically insert a style rule with the styles you provided, using a class name selector based on the hash of those styles.

There's some syntactic fanciness here in the form of an ES6 feature called *tagged templates*.[5] If you put a function directly in front of a template string (the kind delimited by backticks), that function is called with the template string as an argument.

In the case of Img, you could use the normal function call syntax, since the string with the styles is a constant. Where the tagged template syntax unlocks new possibilities is when the string has interpolations (the ${...} syntax): each piece of the interpolated string is passed in to the function as a separate argument. That gives the tag function the chance to process interpolated variables. As we'll soon see, styled-components takes advantage of this power.

As soon as you hit save, you should see the difference in your browser. Before, the size of the <img> tag was determined by the image file it loaded. Now, it takes up the full width of its container and has 500px of height. The object-fit: cover rule means that the image keeps its aspect ratio as it expands or contracts to those dimensions, getting clipped as needed.

---

5. https://developer.mozilla.org/en-US/docs/Web/JavaScript/Reference/Template_literals#Tagged_templates

Why 500px? Really, the height of the image should be determined by the app rendering the carousel component. So let's make these styles dynamic:

```
// src/CarouselSlide.js
import React from 'react';
import PropTypes from 'prop-types';
import styled from 'styled-components';

const Img = styled.img`
  object-fit: cover;
  width: 100%;
❶ height: ${props =>
    typeof props.imgHeight === 'number'
      ? `${props.imgHeight}px`
      : props.imgHeight};
`;

const CarouselSlide = ({
  imgUrl,
  imgHeight,
  description,
  attribution,
  ...rest
}) => (
  <figure {...rest}>
    <Img src={imgUrl} imgHeight={imgHeight} />
    <figcaption>
      <strong>{description}</strong> {attribution}
    </figcaption>
  </figure>
);

CarouselSlide.propTypes = {
❷ imgHeight: PropTypes.oneOfType([PropTypes.number, PropTypes.string]),
  imgUrl: PropTypes.string.isRequired,
  description: PropTypes.node.isRequired,
  attribution: PropTypes.node,
};

❸ CarouselSlide.defaultProps = {
  imgHeight: 500,
};

export default CarouselSlide;
```

❶ This is where styled-components really gets exciting: interpolated values in the style template can be a function of the component's props! Whereas ordinary CSS is static, these styles are completely dynamic. If the imgHeight prop changes, the styles update automatically.

❷ This code declares imgHeight as a prop that can be either a number (indicating a px value) or a string (such as '100vh'). Since it doesn't have isRequired it can also be null; in that case, styled-components would simply omit the height rule from the generated styles.

❸ A React component's defaultProps are used as fallbacks when the prop's given value is undefined. Whereas propTypes are only used during development, defaultProps are always applied.

Note that the src prop passed to Img is passed through to the <img> element it renders. Styled-components filters out props like imgHeight that aren't valid DOM attributes. This means you should be careful what prop names you use for styling. If, for example, we'd named the prop height instead of imgHeight, then it would've been passed down as the height DOM attribute of the <img>.

Right now, imgHeight can be overridden on a slide-by-slide basis, since Carousel passes the whole slide data object down to CarouselSlide as props. But in most cases, the Carousel consumer will want it to have a consistent height. So let's add a prop to Carousel that overrides the default imgHeight on CarouselSlide:

```
// src/Carousel.js
...
export default class Carousel extends React.PureComponent {
  static propTypes = {
    defaultImgHeight: CarouselSlide.propTypes.imgHeight,
    slides: PropTypes.arrayOf(PropTypes.shape(CarouselSlide.propTypes))
      .isRequired,
  };

  static defaultProps = {
    defaultImgHeight: CarouselSlide.defaultProps.imgHeight,
  };
  ...
  render() {
    const { defaultImgHeight, slides, ...rest } = this.props;
    return (
      <div {...rest}>
        <CarouselSlide
          imgHeight={defaultImgHeight}
          {...slides[this.state.slideIndex]}
        />
        <CarouselButton data-action="prev" onClick={this.handlePrevClick}>
          Prev
        </CarouselButton>
        <CarouselButton data-action="next" onClick={this.handleNextClick}>
          Next
        </CarouselButton>
      </div>
    );
  }
}
```

❶ The default value from CarouselSlide's imgHeight is reused as the default value for defaultImgHeight. Functionally, this is redundant, but defaultProps is also commonly used for documentation, as we'll see in Chapter 6, Continuous Integration and Collaboration, on page 147.

❷ Importantly, defaultImgHeight is passed down as imgHeight before the slide data object spread, giving the latter precedence. If it were the other way around, individual slides would be unable to override imgHeight.

If you feel naked without test coverage for all of these changes, you can skip ahead to Testing Styled Components, on page 108, then come back for a detour into styled-components tooling.

So: How did styled-components get our styles into the <img> tag? If you inspect one of the <img> tags in the browser, as in the next screenshot, you'll see that its class attribute is full of gobbledigook. Something like class="sc-bdVaJa hhfYDU". The styled-components library generated these class names for you, and injected a corresponding style rule into a <style> tag in the <head> of the page.

In fact, the <img> element has two classnames generated by styled-components. One of these, the one with the sc- prefix, is a stable class name that styled-components uses for selectors. The other, the one the styles are applied to, is generated from a hash of the styles. In practice, the distinction is just an implementation detail. You should *never, ever* copy any class names generated by styled-components in your code. All generated class names are subject to change.

Having unreadable class names is an unfortunate drawback of styled-components. Luckily, it can be mitigated with help from our good friend Babel.

Better Debugging with the Babel Plugin

We've seen how Babel can bring new features like JSX syntax to JavaScript. But Babel's language-bending abilities can also be used for subtler purposes, tailoring your code to the needs of specific libraries. That's what the official styled-components Babel plugin[6] does. It's a recommended addition for any project that uses styled-components.

Install the plugin with npm:

```
$ npm install --save-dev babel-plugin-styled-components@1.9.2
+ babel-plugin-styled-components@1.9.2
```

Then add it to your Babel config:

```
// .babelrc.js
module.exports = {
  presets: ['@babel/preset-react', '@babel/preset-env'],
  plugins: [
    '@babel/plugin-proposal-class-properties',
    'babel-plugin-styled-components',
  ],
};
```

Restart your dev server, and inspect the element again:

Notice the difference? For one thing, the short class name has changed. (To reiterate: *never* copy class names generated by styled-components into your code!) But more importantly, the formerly sc- prefixed class name is now prefixed with CarouselSlide_Img-. Thanks to the Babel plugin, you can now see the module name (CarouselSlide) and component name (Img) associated with every

---

6. https://www.styled-components.com/docs/tooling#babel-plugin

element styled by styled-components. Note, however, that the short class name is still the one used as the selector.

The Babel plugin also brings efficiency improvements, including the removal of comments and unnecessary whitespace from inside of your template literals, allowing you to write your styles in a human-friendly way without having to worry about the impact on your users' limited bandwidth.

Linting Styles with Stylelint

Once you're used to writing code with a powerful linter like ESLint, doing without a linter can feel like performing on a trampoline without a net: the slightest error can have dramatic effects! That applies to CSS just as it applies to JavaScript. One typo can ruin the look of an entire page. Worse, because browsers vary widely in how they interpret CSS syntax, malformed style rules may work as intended in your preferred development browser but spawn visual bugs in others.

Happily, it's possible to use the popular stylelint[7] CSS linter on styles written for styled-components. Since ESLint ignores the contents of those template literals, the two linters have no trouble peacefully coexisting. In fact, they go together like chocolate and peanut butter.

You'll need a few packages for this: stylelint itself, stylelint-processor-styled-components to tell stylelint which parts of the file to read, stylelint-config-recommended to enable a reasonable set of default rules,[8] and stylelint-config-styled-components to disable some rules that don't apply in the land of styled-components.[9] Install them as dev dependencies:

```
$ npm install --save-dev stylelint@9.9.0 \
    stylelint-config-styled-components@0.1.1 \
    stylelint-config-recommended@2.1.0 \
    stylelint-processor-styled-components@1.5.1
+ stylelint@9.9.0
+ stylelint-config-styled-components@0.1.1
+ stylelint-config-recommended@2.1.0
+ stylelint-processor-styled-components@1.5.1
```

Then create a .stylelintrc.js file in the project root:

```
ch4/.stylelintrc.js
module.exports = {
  processors: ['stylelint-processor-styled-components'],
```

---

7.   https://github.com/stylelint/stylelint
8.   https://github.com/stylelint/stylelint-config-recommended/blob/2.1.0/index.js
9.   https://github.com/styled-components/stylelint-config-styled-components/blob/master/index.js

```
  extends: [
    'stylelint-config-recommended',
    'stylelint-config-styled-components',
  ],
};
```

And as with ESLint, you'll want to tell the linter to ignore the dist dir:

ch4/.stylelintignore
```
dist/
```

One more step: add stylelint to the project's lint script. To keep the line length in package.json manageable, split the script into two parts. Call the existing script lint:js, call the stylelint script lint:css, and run them both from the lint script:

ch4/package.json
```
"scripts": {
  "test": "jest",
  "lint:js": "eslint . && prettier-eslint --list-different **/*.js",
  "lint:css": "stylelint **/*.js",
  "lint": "npm run lint:js && npm run lint:css",
  "format": "prettier-eslint --write **/*.js",
  "build": "webpack --config webpack.config.js",
  "dev": "webpack-dev-server --config webpack.config.js --open"
},
```

❶ By default, stylelint doesn't know what kind of files to look at. The glob argument **/*.js tells it to look at the project's JS files.

There should be no output (aside from npm's) if you run the script, indicating that everything is copacetic right now:

```
$ npm run lint

> test-driven-carousel@1.0.0 lint /Users/tburnham/code/test-driven-carousel
> npm run lint:js && npm run lint:css

> test-driven-carousel@1.0.0 lint:js /Users/tburnham/code/test-driven-carousel
> eslint . && prettier-eslint --list-different **/*.js

> test-driven-carousel@1.0.0 lint:css /Users/tburnham/code/test-driven-carousel
> stylelint **/*.js
```

If you're using VS Code, you'll want to install the stylelint extension by Shinnosuke Watanabe[10] to automatically lint as you type.

From now on, any style code you write will enjoy the benefits of linter coverage. Make a commit:

```
:wrench: Initial stylelint setup
```

---

10. https://marketplace.visualstudio.com/items?itemName=shinnn.stylelint

The stylelint configuration here is just a starting point. For a complete list of rules supported by stylelint that you might want to add to your project, check the official docs.[11]

Default Props in Shallow Tests

This book advocates testing components in isolation (see Mantra: Test One Piece at a Time, on page 87), and the example code given here is written with that principle in mind. Nevertheless, that principle was violated in this chapter, when the addition of defaultProps to the CarouselSlide component broke a test against the Carousel component. How alarmed should you be?

Not very. defaultProps is a singular exception to the rule that code from components other than the one being tested is not executed during shallow testing. propType validation also occurs on all components in the shallow render tree, so you'll see console errors when a shallowly rendered component passes invalid props down.

Testing Styled Components

Let's check how our tests are doing, starting with Carousel:

```
$ npx jest src/tests/Carousel.test.js
 FAIL  src/tests/Carousel.test.js
  Carousel
    ✓ renders a <div> (5ms)
    ✓ has an initial `slideIndex` of 0 (1ms)
    ✓ renders a CarouselButton labeled "Prev" (1ms)
    ✓ renders a CarouselButton labeled "Next"
    ✗ renders the current slide as a CarouselSlide (12ms)
    with a middle slide selected
      ✓ decrements `slideIndex` when Prev is clicked (4ms)
      ✓ increments `slideIndex` when Next is clicked (1ms)
    with the first slide selected
      ✓ wraps `slideIndex` to the max value when Prev is clicked
    with the last slide selected
      ✓ wraps `slideIndex` to the min value when Next is clicked (1ms)

  ● Carousel › renders the current slide as a CarouselSlide

    expect(received).toEqual(expected)

    Expected value to equal:
      {"attribution": "Uno Pizzeria", "description": "Slide 1",
       "imgUrl": "https://example.com/slide1.png"}
    Received:
      {"Img": ...}
```

Currently, the test implicitly assumes that CarouselSlide only has the props it receives from Carousel. That assumption no longer holds now that CarouselSlide has default props. Let's update the test to account for those:

```
// src/tests/Carousel.test.js
...
it('renders the current slide as a CarouselSlide', () => {
  let slideProps;
  slideProps = wrapper.find(CarouselSlide).props();
  expect(slideProps).toEqual({
    ...CarouselSlide.defaultProps,
    ...slides[0],
  });
  wrapper.setState({ slideIndex: 1 });
  slideProps = wrapper.find(CarouselSlide).props();
  expect(slideProps).toEqual({
    ...CarouselSlide.defaultProps,
    ...slides[1],
  });
})...
```

Now move on to the CarouselSlide tests:

```
$ npx jest src/tests/CarouselSlide.test.js
 FAIL  src/tests/CarouselSlide.test.js
  ● CarouselSlide › renders an <img> and a <figcaption> as children

    expect(received).toBe(expected) // Object.is equality

    Expected: "img"
    Received: {"$$typeof": Symbol(react.forward_ref), "attrs": [], ...}

    Difference:

      Comparing two different types of values. Expected string but received
      object.

      20 |
      21 |   it('renders an <img> and a <figcaption> as children', () => {
    > 22 |     expect(wrapper.childAt(0).type()).toBe('img');
         |
                                   ^
```

This is a longwinded way of saying that the first child of the CarouselSlide wrapper element is no longer an <img> element. Instead, it's an instance of the Img component. That component does render an <img> element, but since this is a shallow test of CarouselSlide, the behavior of other components is treated as an unknown.

The problem is we now have two components defined in CarouselSlide.js: CarouselSlide, and the locally defined Img component. We need to expose Img so we can reference the component in tests. For reasons that will become clear

in the next section, let's expose Img by making it a prop. That is, CarouselSlide
will take a prop named Img, and the existing Img component will be the default
value of that prop. This will give us our final CarouselSlide.js for the chapter:

```
ch4/src/CarouselSlide.js
import React from 'react';
import PropTypes from 'prop-types';
import styled from 'styled-components';

const DefaultImg = styled.img`
  object-fit: cover;
  width: 100%;
  height: ${props =>
    typeof props.imgHeight === 'number'
      ? `${props.imgHeight}px`
      : props.imgHeight};
`;

const CarouselSlide = ({
  Img,
  imgUrl,
  imgHeight,
  description,
  attribution,
  ...rest
}) => (
  <figure {...rest}>
    <Img src={imgUrl} imgHeight={imgHeight} />
    <figcaption>
      <strong>{description}</strong> {attribution}
    </figcaption>
  </figure>
);

CarouselSlide.propTypes = {
  Img: PropTypes.elementType,
  imgHeight: PropTypes.oneOfType([PropTypes.number, PropTypes.string]),
  imgUrl: PropTypes.string.isRequired,
  description: PropTypes.node.isRequired,
  attribution: PropTypes.node,
};

CarouselSlide.defaultProps = {
  Img: DefaultImg,
  imgHeight: 500,
};

export default CarouselSlide;
```

❶ PropTypes.elementType, newly added in prop-types@15.7.0, validates that the prop
is a valid argument to React.createElement: either the name of a DOM element
(such as "div"), or a component.

Exposing the Img component provides a direct solution to the failing type() test:

```
// src/tests/CarouselSlide.test.js
...
it('renders props.Img and a <figcaption> as children', () => {
  expect(wrapper.childAt(0).type()).toBe(CarouselSlide.defaultProps.Img);
  expect(wrapper.childAt(1).type()).toBe('figcaption');
});
...
```

With that fix in place, there's one remaining CarouselSlide test failure:

```
$ npx jest
 PASS  src/tests/CarouselButton.test.js
 FAIL  src/tests/CarouselSlide.test.js
  ● CarouselSlide › passes `imgUrl` through to the <img>

    Method "props" is only meant to be run on a single node. 0 found instead.

      28 |     wrapper.setProps({ imgUrl });
      29 |     const img = wrapper.find('img');
    > 30 |     expect(img.prop('src')).toBe(imgUrl);
         |              ^
```

The error message is Enzyme's way of telling us that wrapper.find('img') didn't match anything. Recall that we're using shallow rendering, which means that find() only looks at the React tree that CarouselSlide's render() method returns. Before this chapter, render() returned a tree that contained an <img> element. Now it doesn't. Instead, it returns a component whose render() method returns an <img> element.

The fix is the same as the type() test—substitute the Img component for 'img':

```
// src/tests/CarouselSlide.test.js
...
it('passes `imgUrl` through to props.Img', () => {
  const imgUrl = 'https://example.com/image.png';
  wrapper.setProps({ imgUrl });
  const img = wrapper.find(CarouselSlide.defaultProps.Img);
  expect(img.prop('src')).toBe(imgUrl);
});
...
```

Now the CarouselSlide tests are all passing, and the component's coverage is as good as ever. But the Img component itself has no coverage. Although the component is very simple, it's always a good idea to use tests to validate assumptions. Right now, there are two important assumptions here:

1. The imgUrl prop is passed down to an Img instance as the src prop
2. The Img component renders an <img> element with the given src prop

Because we're interested in the DOM output of the component, we should use Enzyme's mount() to test these assumptions instead of shallow():

```
// src/tests/CarouselSlide.test.js
import React from 'react';
import { shallow, mount } from 'enzyme';
import CarouselSlide from '../CarouselSlide';
...
describe('Img', () => {
  let mounted;
  const imgUrl = 'https://example.com/default.jpg';

  beforeEach(() => {
    const Img = CarouselSlide.defaultProps.Img;
    mounted = mount(
      <Img src={imgUrl} imgHeight={500} />
    );
  });

  it('renders an <img> with the given src', () => {
    expect(mounted.containsMatchingElement(<img src={imgUrl} />)).toBe(true);
  });
});
```

Like shallow(), mount() takes a React tree, renders it, and returns a wrapper that lets you make queries about that tree. Unlike shallow(), mount() fully renders the tree to the DOM. The Enzyme wrapper's containsMatchingElement() method conveniently answers all of our questions about the component in one go. For more information on mount(), check out the official docs.[12]

A word of caution about mount(): by providing the entire DOM tree rendered by a component, including DOM elements produced by nested components, mount() ignores the principle that components should be tested in isolation (see Mantra: Test One Piece at a Time, on page 87). In this case, though, the component being tested comes from a third-party library. What goes on under the hood isn't really our concern; we just want to know that it creates the markup its API promised. Used sparingly, mount() tests like this one can be a healthy supplement to shallow() tests, particularly when using React components from another project.

Now your tests cover everything we need to know about the markup that CarouselSlide renders. The only thing left to test is the styles themselves. Commit your work before moving on:

```
:white_check_mark: Update tests for styled-components
```

---

12. https://airbnb.io/enzyme/docs/api/mount.html

Making Assertions About Styles

To make assertions about the styles that styled-components generates, you'll need the Jest styled-components plugin.[13] Install jest-styled-components with npm:

```
$ npm install --save-dev jest-styled-components@6.3.1
+ jest-styled-components@6.3.1
```

Then you'll need to bring in the plugin before running your tests:

ch4/src/tests/jestSetup.js
```
import Adapter from 'enzyme-adapter-react-16';
import { configure } from 'enzyme';
➤ import 'jest-styled-components';

configure({ adapter: new Adapter() });
```

Now you have a new assertion at your disposal, toHaveStyleRule(). Add a test to the describe('Img') block to make sure that the expected styled.img styles are coming through:

```
// src/tests/CarouselSlide.test.js
...
describe('Img', () => {
  ...
➤  it('has the expected static styles', () => {
➤    expect(mounted).toHaveStyleRule('width', '100%');
➤    expect(mounted).toHaveStyleRule('object-fit', 'cover');
➤  });
});
```

Those tests should all come through green. Now add another test to confirm that the imgHeight prop works as expected. Since the default value is numeric, try a string value:

```
// src/tests/CarouselSlide.test.js
...
describe('Img', () => {
  ...
➤  it('uses imgHeight as the height style property', () => {
➤    expect(mounted).toHaveStyleRule('height', '500px');
➤    mounted.setProps({ imgHeight: 'calc(100vh - 100px)' });
➤    expect(mounted).toHaveStyleRule('height', 'calc(100vh - 100px)');
➤  });
});
```

Once again, all tests should be green. Time for a commit:

```
:white_check_mark: Add style tests for the <img>
```

---

13. https://github.com/styled-components/jest-styled-components

Now let's try out one of styled-components' coolest features: extending styled components. If you pass an existing styled component to styled(), it'll return a new component with the styles from the original component *plus* the new styles. The new styles take precedence, so this is a convenient way to override existing styles and avoid the specificity wars that are endemic in large CSS projects.

Give it a try:

```
// src/tests/CarouselSlide.test.js
import React from 'react';
import { shallow } from 'enzyme';
import CarouselSlide from '../CarouselSlide';
import styled from 'styled-components';
...
describe('Img', () => {
  ...
  it('allows styles to be overridden', () => {
    const TestImg = styled(CarouselSlide.defaultProps.Img)`
      width: auto;
      height: auto;
      object-fit: fill;
    `;

    mounted = mount(
      <CarouselSlide
        Img={TestImg}
        imgUrl={imgUrl}
        description="This prop is required"
      />
    );

    expect(mounted.find(TestImg)).toHaveStyleRule('width', 'auto');
    expect(mounted.find(TestImg)).toHaveStyleRule('height', 'auto');
    expect(mounted.find(TestImg)).toHaveStyleRule('object-fit', 'fill');
  });
});
```

Now you can see why Img is exposed as a prop. Before, the only way for the CarouselSlide consumer to alter the styles on the <img> element (aside from height) would've been to craft a CSS rule that targets it with an img element selector. But with the Img prop, the consumer can take the default component, extend it with new styles, and replace the original. Not only does that make it easy to override the styles, it also gives them a hook for inserting event handlers, DOM attributes, or additional markup. One prop, infinite extensibility.

As it stands, someone using Carousel who wants to modify <img> would have to set Img individually on each slide data object. It'd be convenient to be able to set a single prop on Carousel for modifying Img across the board, similar to the defaultImgHeight prop.

Let's switch back into TDD mode. Add some tests for both the as-yet-undefined defaultImg prop and the existing defaultImgHeight prop:

```
// src/tests/Carousel.test.js
...
describe('Carousel', () => {
  ...
➤  it('passes defaultImg and defaultImgHeight to the CarouselSlide', () => {
➤    const defaultImg = () => 'test';
➤    const defaultImgHeight = 1234;
➤    wrapper.setProps({ defaultImg, defaultImgHeight });
➤    expect(wrapper.find(CarouselSlide).prop('Img')).toBe(defaultImg);
➤    expect(wrapper.find(CarouselSlide).prop('imgHeight')).toBe(
➤      defaultImgHeight
➤    );
➤  });
➤
➤  it('allows individual slides to override Img and imgHeight', () => {
➤    const Img = () => 'test';
➤    const imgHeight = 1234;
➤    wrapper.setProps({ slides: [{ ...slides[0], Img, imgHeight }] });
➤    expect(wrapper.find(CarouselSlide).prop('Img')).toBe(Img);
➤    expect(wrapper.find(CarouselSlide).prop('imgHeight')).toBe(imgHeight);
➤  });
});
```

Then move to the implementation:

```
// src/Carousel.js
...
export default class Carousel extends React.PureComponent {
  static propTypes = {
➤    defaultImg: CarouselSlide.propTypes.Img,
    defaultImgHeight: CarouselSlide.propTypes.imgHeight,
    slides: PropTypes.arrayOf(PropTypes.shape(CarouselSlide.propTypes))
      .isRequired,
  };

  static defaultProps = {
➤    defaultImg: CarouselSlide.defaultProps.Img,
    defaultImgHeight: CarouselSlide.defaultProps.imgHeight,
  };
  ...
  render() {
➤    const { defaultImg, defaultImgHeight, slides, ...rest } = this.props;
    return (
➤      <div {...rest}>
➤        <CarouselSlide
➤          Img={defaultImg}
```

```
➤          imgHeight={defaultImgHeight}
➤          {...slides[this.state.slideIndex]}
➤        />
➤        <CarouselButton data-action="prev" onClick={this.handlePrevClick}>
➤          Prev
➤        </CarouselButton>
➤        <CarouselButton data-action="next" onClick={this.handleNextClick}>
➤          Next
➤        </CarouselButton>
➤      </div>
      );
    }
  }
```

And commit:

```
:sparkles: Add prop for extending the <img> component
```

At this point, let's pause and reflect on what it means to have adequate test coverage for styles. In this section, we created a toHaveStyleRule() assertion for every style rule. For dynamic rules like height, that's useful: any time props are converted into something the user can see, it's worth making sure that conversion works as expected. But for static rules, toHaveStyleRule() is close to being a truism: "Test that x is x."

Still, it'd be nice to have some kind of sanity check when restyling components. What if you had a tool that automatically generated a diff of the component's styles before and after, allowing you to review and confirm that your changes reflect your intent? In the next section, you'll learn how to do just that using a Jest feature called *snapshots*.

Taking Jest Snapshots

When you think of testing, you probably picture a list of assertions about your code, a sort of checklist of its functionality. Up to this point, all of the tests in this book have fit that description. But sometimes a picture is worth a thousand words. Or in this case, a piece of content generated by your code can be worth a thousand assertions. Seeing a diff of that content can bring your attention to problems you might never have thought to write an assertion for.

For our purposes, the content we're interested in snapshotting is the DOM generated by CarouselSlide, along with the styles generated by styled-components. To do that, you'll need to install one more package, enzyme-to-json:

```
$ npm install --save-dev enzyme-to-json@3.3.5
+ enzyme-to-json@3.3.5
```

enzyme-to-json takes the trees from Enzyme wrappers and converts them to the JSON format used for Jest snapshot testing, a process known as serialization. To tell Jest to use the package, declare it in the Jest config:

```
ch4/jest.config.js
module.exports = {
  setupTestFrameworkScriptFile: './src/tests/jestSetup.js',
  snapshotSerializers: ['enzyme-to-json/serializer'],
};
```

If you are using Wallaby.js, be sure that you restart it to bring in the updated Jest config.

Now add a test with a new assertion (courtesy of the jest-styled-components plugin), toMatchSnapshot():

```
// src/tests/CarouselSlide.test.js
...
describe('CarouselSlide', () => {
  ...
  it('renders correctly', () => {
    wrapper.setProps({
      description: 'Description',
      attribution: 'Attribution',
    });
    expect(wrapper).toMatchSnapshot();
  });
});
...
```

Then try running it:

```
$ npx jest
 PASS  src/tests/CarouselButton.test.js
 PASS  src/tests/Carousel.test.js
 PASS  src/tests/CarouselSlide.test.js
 › 1 snapshot written.

Snapshot Summary
 › 1 snapshot written from 1 test suite.
```

Jest created a new directory, src/tests/__snapshots__, with one file:

```
// src/tests/__snapshots__/CarouselSlide.test.js.snap
// Jest Snapshot v1, https://goo.gl/fbAQLP

exports[`CarouselSlide renders correctly 1`] = `
<figure>
  <CarouselSlide__DefaultImg
    imgHeight={500}
    src="https://example.com/default.jpg"
  />
```

```
      <figcaption>
        <strong>
          Description
        </strong>

        Attribution
      </figcaption>
    </figure>
  `;
```

This provides a nice, clear picture of what CarouselSlide (shallowly) renders. Try taking a snapshot of the Img component, too:

```
// src/tests/CarouselSlide.test.js
...
describe('Img', () => {
  ...
  it('renders correctly', () => {
    expect(mounted.find('img')).toMatchSnapshot();
  });
});
```

Run the test and you'll see another snapshot in the same file:

```
// src/tests/__snapshots__/CarouselSlide.test.js.snap
...
exports[`Img renders correctly 1`] = `
.c0 {
  object-fit: cover;
  width: 100%;
  height: 500px;
}

<img
  className="c0"
  src="https://example.com/default.jpg"
/>
`;
```

Beautiful! Now you can see that the generated markup is just as expected, and that the <img> element receives a className that confers the expected styles. (As is always the case with styled-components, the particular class name—c0 here—is arbitrary.)

These two snapshots are an excellent substitute for several of the existing tests about CarouselSlide's markup. Removing those rather rigid tests will help make it easier to change the component's markup in the future: instead of making changes to multiple failing tests, you'll only have to confirm that the new snapshots reflect your intent.

Pruning the tests that are redundant with the snapshots yields the final CarouselSlide.test.js for this chapter:

ch4/src/tests/CarouselSlide.test.js

```
import React from 'react';
import { shallow, mount } from 'enzyme';
import CarouselSlide from '../CarouselSlide';

describe('CarouselSlide', () => {
  let wrapper;

  beforeEach(() => {
    wrapper = shallow(
      <CarouselSlide
        imgUrl="https://example.com/default.jpg"
        description="Default test image"
      />
    );
  });

  it('renders correctly', () => {
    wrapper.setProps({
      description: 'Description',
      attribution: 'Attribution',
    });
    expect(wrapper).toMatchSnapshot();
  });

  it('passes other props through to the <figure>', () => {
    const style = {};
    const onClick = () => {};
    const className = 'my-carousel-slide';
    wrapper.setProps({ style, onClick, className });
    expect(wrapper.prop('style')).toBe(style);
    expect(wrapper.prop('onClick')).toBe(onClick);
    expect(wrapper.prop('className')).toBe(className);
  });
});

describe('Img', () => {
  let mounted;
  const imgUrl = 'https://example.com/default.jpg';

  beforeEach(() => {
    const Img = CarouselSlide.defaultProps.Img;
    mounted = mount(
      <Img src={imgUrl} imgHeight={500} />
    );
  });

  it('renders correctly', () => {
    expect(mounted.find('img')).toMatchSnapshot();
  });
```

```
  it('uses imgHeight as the height style property', () => {
    expect(mounted).toHaveStyleRule('height', '500px');
    mounted.setProps({ imgHeight: 'calc(100vh - 100px)' });
    expect(mounted).toHaveStyleRule('height', 'calc(100vh - 100px)');
  });
});
```

From now on, every time you run your tests, Jest will generate new snapshots to compare to the old ones. If the two are identical, the toMatchSnapshot() assertion passes. But what happens if they're different? Try changing, say, the object-fit style rule from cover to contain:

```
$ npx jest
 PASS  src/tests/CarouselButton.test.js
 PASS  src/tests/Carousel.test.js
 FAIL  src/tests/CarouselSlide.test.js
  ● Img › renders correctly

    expect(value).toMatchSnapshot()

    Received value does not match stored snapshot "Img renders correctly 1".

    - Snapshot
    + Received

    @@ -1,8 +1,8 @@
      .c0 {
        width: 100%;
    -   object-fit: cover;
    +   object-fit: contain;
      }

      <img
        className="c0"
        src="https://example.com/default.jpg"

      43 |
      44 |   it('renders correctly', () => {
    > 45 |     expect(mounted.find('img')).toMatchSnapshot();
         |                                 ^
      46 |   });
      47 |
      48 |   it('uses imgHeight as the height style property', () => {

      at Object.toMatchSnapshot (src/tests/CarouselSlide.test.js:45:33)

 › 1 snapshot failed.
Snapshot Summary
 › 1 snapshot failed from 1 test suite. Inspect your code changes or run
 `npx jest -u` to update them.
```

When a toMatchSnapshot() assertion fails, Jest treats that as a test failure and shows you a diff of the snapshot. The snapshot on disk remains unchanged.

To confirm that your change is intentional, you run the tests again with the -u (short for --updateSnapshot) flag, causing all snapshots to be overwritten.

> ### Snapshot Testing in Wallaby.js
>
> Wallaby offers excellent support for snapshot testing, including the ability to view snapshot diffs side-by-side in your editor and update snapshots individually. For details, check the official docs.[a]
>
> _____
>
> a.   https://wallabyjs.com/docs/integration/jest.html#snapshot-testing

This snapshot process may feel strange at first. Unit tests are normally automated. Snapshot testing, by contrast, requires human intervention: on its own, the machine can't determine whether the test should pass or not. That brings human error into the equation. In practice, this downside is mitigated by the fact that snapshots are version controlled. If a pull request contains an unwanted change that's reflected in a snapshot that the author carelessly updated, everyone reviewing that pull request will see the snapshot diff and have a chance to raise a red flag.

Speaking of version control, it's time to make your final commit for this chapter:

```
:white_check_mark: Add snapshot tests for CarouselSlide
```

This concludes our tour of styled-components and testing. We only got around to styling one element, the <img>, so there's lots left to do! As an exercise for this chapter, try adding some finishing touches to the carousel. Play around with different styles for the caption, the buttons, and the overall layout. When you feel satisfied with your work, be sure to add a snapshot test for each element, then breathe a sigh of relief that your styles are safe from regressions.

Mantra: Actively Seek Feedback

The spirit of TDD extends beyond writing tests before you write code. The goal of TDD is to set up a constructive feedback loop for yourself, to identify potential problems quickly and give yourself the freedom to explore potential improvements. Tests are only a means to that end. Sometimes, you'll want to set tests aside and focus on other sources of feedback. The important thing is to always think ahead: before you start writing a piece of code, ask yourself what the most valuable feedback you could receive for that code would be. Then take steps to make it a reality. In other words: *"actively seek feedback."*

In this chapter, you learned how to use the styled-components library to create components with integrated, extensible, fully testable styles. You also added some powerful new tools to your belt, including webpack-dev-server, stylelint, and Jest snapshots. Each of these tools give you more options for seeking feedback as you work. Whenever you find yourself stuck, ask if you might be focusing on the wrong kind of feedback.

In the next chapter, you'll learn about higher-order components (HOCs), a technique for making React code reusable and keeping individual components from growing too complex.

CHAPTER 5

Refactoring with Higher-Order Components

The power of React is that it allows you to express web apps in individual units called components. But the rules for assigning different bits of functionality to different components aren't always clear. In principle, any React app could be expressed as a single monolithic component. Or at the opposite extreme, every DOM element in the page could be managed by its own micro-component.

A good rule of thumb is that components should be built in such a way that each component has only one job. Components with multiple responsibilities are a good candidate for being split up. These distinctions are intuitive, not technical—no automated process is going to tell you whether a component has multiple responsibilities. Still, thinking in these terms will help you as you work to keep code manageable. The more complex an individual component is, the harder it'll be to make changes to it.

This chapter is about splitting up complex components into simpler pieces using a pattern called *higher-order components* (HOCs). You'll add new functionality to the carousel component from the previous chapter while actually simplifying the core component by extracting some of its logic to an HOC. And you'll learn how to use the React Devtools to see how different components are interacting in your browser.

Making Higher-Order Components

In the abstract, a higher-order component is defined as any function that takes a component and returns another component. Typically, the component returned by the HOC function is a wrapper around the original component that adds functionality. Here's a simple example:

```
const BindProps = (Component, boundProps) => {
  const ComponentWithBoundProps = props => (
    <Component {...props} {...boundProps} />
  );
  ComponentWithBoundProps.displayName =
    `BindProps(${Component.displayName || Component.name})`;
  return ComponentWithBoundProps;
};
const CarouselWithTestAttr = BindProps(Carousel, {
  'data-test-id': 'carousel',
});
```

❶ The BindProps HOC takes two arguments, a component and a props object to "bind" to that component.

❷ Since the boundProps passed to the HOC are spread into the component after the props passed directly, the boundProps take precedence.

❸ displayName is a special property that gives React components a name for debugging purposes. We haven't had to deal with it so far because JavaScript functions and classes have a name property that usually works as a fallback. But for a dynamically generated component like this one, you'll need to set the name manually. Using a name of the form "HOC(Component)" is a common convention.

❹ Here BindProps is used to generate a component that behaves exactly like Carousel, except that it will always receive data-test-id="carousel".

In the next section, you'll build an HOC to manage an index, like the slideIndex in Carousel. Then you'll refactor Carousel to make it a stateless component using that HOC.

Creating a Higher-Order Component

Open the test-driven-carousel project from the previous chapter and take a look at the Carousel component. In addition to rendering a somewhat complex DOM tree, it also has one piece of state and two event handlers that manipulate that state. Let's try building an HOC that encapsulates that logic.

Well-implemented HOCs tend to be highly reusable, and this one will be no exception. It'll manage the state for any component that has an "index" prop, meaning a number that can go from 0 up to some limit. Call it HasIndex. Start with a minimal dummy implementation that you can run tests against:

```
// src/HasIndex.js
import React from 'react';

export default (Component, indexPropName) =>
  class ComponentWithIndex extends React.PureComponent {
    static displayName =
      `HasIndex(${Component.displayName || Component.name})`;

    render() {
      return <Component {...this.props} />;
    }
  };
```

To replace the slideIndex logic in Carousel, we need HasIndex to provide three props to the wrapped component: the index itself (with the given indexPropName), an increment function, and a decrement function. To support wrap-around, the increment and decrement functions should accept an upper bound argument. Write a test suite with those requirements:

```
// src/tests/HasIndex.test.js
import React from 'react';
import { shallow } from 'enzyme';
import HasIndex from '../HasIndex';

describe('HasIndex()', () => {
  const MockComponent = () => null;
  MockComponent.displayName = 'MockComponent';
  const MockComponentWithIndex = HasIndex(MockComponent, 'index');

  it('has the expected displayName', () => {
    expect(MockComponentWithIndex.displayName).toBe(
      'HasIndex(MockComponent)'
    );
  });

  let wrapper;
  beforeEach(() => {
    wrapper = shallow(<MockComponentWithIndex />);
  });

  it('has an initial `index` state of 0', () => {
    expect(wrapper.state('index')).toBe(0);
  });

  it('passes the `index` state down as the `index` prop', () => {
    expect(wrapper.prop('index')).toBe(0);
    wrapper.setState({ index: 1 });
    expect(wrapper.prop('index')).toBe(1);
  });
```

```
  it('has an `index` state of 2 on decrement from 3', () => {
    wrapper.setState({ index: 3 });
    wrapper.prop('indexDecrement')();
    expect(wrapper.state('index')).toBe(2);
  });

  it('has an `index` state of 1 on increment', () => {
    wrapper.prop('indexIncrement')();
    expect(wrapper.state('index')).toBe(1);
  });

  it('has the max `index` state on decrement from 0', () => {
    wrapper.setState({ index: 0 });
    wrapper.prop('indexDecrement')(3);
    expect(wrapper.state('index')).toBe(2);
  });

  it('has the min `index` state on increment from the max', () => {
    wrapper.setState({ index: 2 });
    wrapper.prop('indexIncrement')(3);
    expect(wrapper.state('index')).toBe(0);
  });
});
```

Then try modifying the implementation to meet those requirements. You should end up with something like this:

```
// src/HasIndex.js
import React from 'react';

export default (Component, indexPropName) =>
➤  class ComponentWithIndex extends React.PureComponent {
➤    static displayName = `HasIndex(${Component.displayName ||
➤      Component.name})`;
➤
➤    state = {
➤      index: 0,
➤    };
➤
➤    handleDecrement = upperBound => {
➤      this.setState(({ index }) => {
➤        const newIndex = upperBound
➤          ? (index + upperBound - 1) % upperBound
➤          : index - 1;
➤        return {
➤          index: newIndex,
➤        };
➤      });
➤    };
➤
```

```
    handleIncrement = upperBound => {
      this.setState(({ index }) => {
        const newIndex = upperBound ? (index + 1) % upperBound : index + 1;
        return {
          index: newIndex,
        };
      });
    };

    render() {
      const indexProps = {
        [indexPropName]: this.state.index,
        [`${indexPropName}Decrement`]: this.handleDecrement,
        [`${indexPropName}Increment`]: this.handleIncrement,
      };
      return <Component {...this.props} {...indexProps} />;
    }
  };
```

Now that all of HasIndex's tests are green, this would be a good time to commit your work:

```
:sparkles: Add HasIndex HOC
```

Refactoring with Higher-Order Components

With HasIndex, you can now make Carousel a stateless component. Instead of having an initialState and performing setState operations, Carousel will receive slideIndex as a prop and use the slideIndexDecrement and slideIndexIncrement props to update that value.

This change will make the "core" of Carousel simpler (especially as you add new features related to the slide index), but it complicates the shallow testing story. Up to now, Carousel has been a single component that contains all of its own logic. Now it will, in effect, be two components. You're going to need three types of test to achieve full coverage:

1. Tests for the component generated by HasIndex (which you already have)
2. Tests for the core Carousel component
3. Tests to ensure that the core and the HOC are properly wired together

Start by modifying Carousel.js so that it exports both the core Carousel component and, as the default export, a HasIndex-wrapped version:

```
// src/Carousel.js
import React from 'react';
import PropTypes from 'prop-types';
import CarouselButton from './CarouselButton';
import CarouselSlide from './CarouselSlide';
➤ import HasIndex from './HasIndex';

➤ export class Carousel extends React.PureComponent {
    ...
  }

➤ export default HasIndex(Carousel, 'slideIndex');
```

In Carousel.test.js, you'll need to import and test both components. Since the component wrapped with HasIndex is the one that your library's users will consume, import it as Carousel, and import the unmodified component as CoreCarousel:

```
// src/tests/Carousel.test.js
import React from 'react';
import { shallow } from 'enzyme';
➤ import Carousel, { Carousel as CoreCarousel } from '../Carousel';
import CarouselButton from '../CarouselButton';
import CarouselSlide from '../CarouselSlide';

describe('Carousel', () => {
  ...
➤   describe('component with HOC', () => {
➤     // Tests against Carousel will go here
➤   });
➤
➤   describe('core component', () => {
➤     // Tests against CoreCarousel will go here
➤   });
  });
```

The tests in the describe('component with HOC', ...) block only need to verify that the core component is correctly wrapped by HasIndex, since you already have solid test coverage for HasIndex itself. An effective way to confirm that is to check that the core component receives both the props generated *by* the wrapper component and the props passed *to* the wrapped component:

```
// src/tests/Carousel.test.js
...
describe('component with HOC', () => {
➤   let wrapper;
➤
➤   beforeEach(() => {
➤     wrapper = shallow(<Carousel slides={slides} />);
➤   });
➤
```

```
    it('sets slideIndex={0} on the core component', () => {
      expect(wrapper.find(CoreCarousel).prop('slideIndex')).toBe(0);
    });

    it('passes `slides` down to the core component', () => {
      expect(wrapper.find(CoreCarousel).prop('slides')).toBe(slides);
    });
  });
  ...
```

The describe('core component', ...) block should be essentially the same as the old
Carousel tests, except the tests need to deal with slideIndex as a prop instead of state:

```
// src/tests/Carousel.test.js
...
describe('core component', () => {
  const slideIndexDecrement = jest.fn();
  const slideIndexIncrement = jest.fn();
  let wrapper;

  beforeEach(() => {
    wrapper = shallow(
      <CoreCarousel
        slides={slides}
        slideIndex={0}
        slideIndexDecrement={slideIndexDecrement}
        slideIndexIncrement={slideIndexIncrement}
      />
    );
  });

  it('renders a <div>', () => {
    expect(wrapper.type()).toBe('div');
  });

  it('renders a CarouselButton labeled "Prev"', () => {
    expect(
      wrapper
        .find(CarouselButton)
        .at(0)
        .prop('children')
    ).toBe('Prev');
  });

  it('renders a CarouselButton labeled "Next"', () => {
    expect(
      wrapper
        .find(CarouselButton)
        .at(1)
        .prop('children')
    ).toBe('Next');
  });
```

```
➤  it('renders the current slide as a CarouselSlide', () => {
➤    let slideProps;
➤    slideProps = wrapper.find(CarouselSlide).props();
➤    expect(slideProps).toEqual({
➤      ...CarouselSlide.defaultProps,
➤      ...slides[0],
➤    });
➤    wrapper.setProps({ slideIndex: 1 });
➤    slideProps = wrapper.find(CarouselSlide).props();
➤    expect(slideProps).toEqual({
➤      ...CarouselSlide.defaultProps,
➤      ...slides[1],
➤    });
➤  });
➤
➤  it('decrements `slideIndex` when Prev is clicked', () => {
➤    wrapper.find('[data-action="prev"]').simulate('click');
❷    expect(slideIndexDecrement).toHaveBeenCalledWith(slides.length);
➤  });
➤
➤  it('increments `slideIndex` when Next is clicked', () => {
➤    wrapper.find('[data-action="next"]').simulate('click');
➤    expect(slideIndexIncrement).toHaveBeenCalledWith(slides.length);
➤  });

  it('passes defaultImg and defaultImgHeight to the CarouselSlide', () => {
    const defaultImg = () => 'test';
    const defaultImgHeight = 1234;
    wrapper.setProps({ defaultImg, defaultImgHeight });
    expect(wrapper.find(CarouselSlide).prop('Img')).toBe(defaultImg);
    expect(wrapper.find(CarouselSlide).prop('imgHeight')).toBe(
      defaultImgHeight
    );
  });

  it('allows individual slides to override Img and imgHeight', () => {
    const Img = () => 'test';
    const imgHeight = 1234;
    wrapper.setProps({ slides: [{ ...slides[0], Img, imgHeight }] });
    expect(wrapper.find(CarouselSlide).prop('Img')).toBe(Img);
    expect(wrapper.find(CarouselSlide).prop('imgHeight')).toBe(imgHeight);
  });
});
...
```

❶ jest.fn() creates a *mock function*, a function that keeps track of calls to itself.[1]

❷ expect(mockFunction).toHaveBeenCalledWith() is an assertion that verifies that mockFunction was called with the given arguments.

---

1. https://jestjs.io/docs/en/mock-functions

With the tests updated, you're ready to implement the refactoring:

```
// src/Carousel.js
import React from 'react';
import PropTypes from 'prop-types';
import CarouselButton from './CarouselButton';
import CarouselSlide from './CarouselSlide';
import HasIndex from './HasIndex';

export class Carousel extends React.PureComponent {
  static propTypes = {
    defaultImg: CarouselSlide.propTypes.Img,
    defaultImgHeight: CarouselSlide.propTypes.imgHeight,
    slideIndex: PropTypes.number.isRequired,
    slideIndexDecrement: PropTypes.func.isRequired,
    slideIndexIncrement: PropTypes.func.isRequired,
    slides: PropTypes.arrayOf(PropTypes.shape(CarouselSlide.propTypes))
      .isRequired,
  };

  static defaultProps = {
    defaultImg: CarouselSlide.defaultProps.Img,
    defaultImgHeight: CarouselSlide.defaultProps.imgHeight,
  };

  handlePrevClick = () => {
    const { slideIndexDecrement, slides } = this.props;
    slideIndexDecrement(slides.length);
  };

  handleNextClick = () => {
    const { slideIndexIncrement, slides } = this.props;
    slideIndexIncrement(slides.length);
  };

  render() {
    const {
      defaultImg,
      defaultImgHeight,
      slideIndex,
      slideIndexDecrement: _slideIndexDecrement,
      slideIndexIncrement: _slideIndexIncrement,
      slides,
      ...rest
    } = this.props;
    return (
      <div {...rest}>
        <CarouselSlide
          Img={defaultImg}
          imgHeight={defaultImgHeight}
          {...slides[slideIndex]}
        />
```

```
        <CarouselButton data-action="prev" onClick={this.handlePrevClick}>
          Prev
        </CarouselButton>
        <CarouselButton data-action="next" onClick={this.handleNextClick}>
          Next
        </CarouselButton>
      </div>
    );
  }
}

export default HasIndex(Carousel, 'slideIndex');
```

❶ We don't want slideIndexDecrement and slideIndexIncrement to be part of the rest props, since those are passed through to the DOM. Instead, this code pulls them out as variables prefixed with the underscore character, _. The underscore prefix is a convention that we'll make use of momentarily.

ESLint isn't too happy about the _slideIndexDecrement and _slideIndexIncrement variables this code creates as a side effect of keeping those props out of the rest spread. But this is the best available pattern. So, let's modify the linter rules to ignore unused variables whose names start with an underscore:

```
ch5/.eslintrc.js
module.exports = {
  plugins: ['react'],
  extends: ['eslint:recommended', 'plugin:react/recommended'],
  parser: 'babel-eslint',
  env: {
    node: true,
  },
  rules: {
    quotes: ['error', 'single', { avoidEscape: true }],
    'comma-dangle': ['error', 'always-multiline'],
➤   'no-unused-vars': ['error', { varsIgnorePattern: '^_' }],
  },
};
```

There! The linter is happy. More importantly, you've successfully made Carousel a stateless component, with its state logic extracted to a reusable HOC. Time to commit your work, using the recommended gitmoji for refactoring:

```
:recycle: Replace Carousel state with HasIndex HOC
```

This is a powerful refactoring. In the rest of the chapter, you'll take advantage of this structure to add two new features to Carousel without making any modifications to the core component.

The Controllable Pattern

Components in React are commonly described as *controlled* or *uncontrolled* with respect to some variable. If that variable is passed down to it through props, the component is controlled. If that variable is managed as state, the component is uncontrolled.

In its original incarnation, Carousel was uncontrolled with respect to slideIndex. With the HasIndex refactoring, the core of Carousel is now controlled, but the overall component—the version of Carousel that this library's users will consume—is still uncontrolled. Nothing outside of Carousel can modify its slideIndex, because that variable is kept in state.

Suppose you removed the HasIndex wrapper to make Carousel controlled. That would make the component more versatile, since the user could change the slideIndex freely. But it would also make it more cumbersome, since the user would have to implement their own slideIndexDecrement and slideIndexIncrement handlers.

What if you could get the best of both worlds? That's what the *controllable* pattern offers. As its name suggests, a controllable component is one that can be optionally controlled. If the user chooses not to control the variable in question, then it functions as an uncontrolled component. The controllable pattern is exemplified by React's own wrappers around form elements, e.g. <input>.

In this section, you will modify HasIndex to make the slideIndex on Carousel controllable.

Implementing Controllable Behaviors

Making Carousel controllable entails accepting a slideIndex prop with the following behavior:

1. If slideIndex is undefined, it continues to function the way it always has, changing slideIndex internally when the Prev/Next buttons are clicked.

2. If slideIndex is defined, it overrides any internal state.

One implication of this is that the Prev/Next buttons will no longer be able to change the effective slideIndex if the prop is set. Instead, they should trigger a change event, conventionally named onSlideIndexChange. This event gives whoever is controlling the Carousel the option to update the slideIndex prop.

This is a common source of confusion, so it bears emphasis: when onSlideIndex-Change is called, it does not necessarily mean that the slideIndex has changed.

Really it can mean two things: in the uncontrolled case, it means slideIndex (the internal value) has changed; in the controlled case, it means slideIndex *would* change if the component were uncontrolled, and the controller has the option to change the slideIndex prop accordingly. A fundamental rule of React is that components have no power to change their own props.

You can express all of these requirements as tests against HasIndex:

ch5/src/tests/HasIndex.test.js

```
import React from 'react';
import { shallow } from 'enzyme';
import HasIndex from '../HasIndex';

describe('HasIndex()', () => {
  const MockComponent = () => null;
  MockComponent.displayName = 'MockComponent';
  const MockComponentWithIndex = HasIndex(MockComponent, 'index');

  it('has the expected displayName', () => {
    expect(MockComponentWithIndex.displayName).toBe(
      'HasIndex(MockComponent)'
    );
  });

  let wrapper;
  beforeEach(() => {
    wrapper = shallow(<MockComponentWithIndex />);
  });
```
❶
```
  it('has initial `index` state equal to the `defaultIndex` prop', () => {
    expect(wrapper.state('index')).toBe(0);
    const wrapper2 = shallow(<MockComponentWithIndex defaultIndex={1} />);
    expect(wrapper2.state('index')).toBe(1);
  });
```
❷
```
  it('always has `index` state equal to the `index` prop', () => {
    const wrapperWithInitialIndex = shallow(
      <MockComponentWithIndex index={1} />
    );
    expect(wrapperWithInitialIndex.state('index')).toBe(1);
    wrapper.setProps({ index: 2 });
    expect(wrapper.state('index')).toBe(2);
  });
```
❸
```
  it('allows `index` state to change if the `index` prop is unset', () => {
    const wrapperWithInitialIndex = shallow(
      <MockComponentWithIndex index={1} />
    );
    wrapperWithInitialIndex.setProps({ index: undefined });
    wrapperWithInitialIndex.setState({ index: 3 });
    expect(wrapperWithInitialIndex.state('index')).toBe(3);
  });
```

```
❹  it('calls `onIndexChange` on decrement/increment', () => {
     const onIndexChange = jest.fn();
     wrapper.setProps({ index: 0, onIndexChange });
     wrapper.prop('indexDecrement')(3);
     expect(onIndexChange).toHaveBeenCalledWith({ target: { value: 2 } });
     wrapper.prop('indexIncrement')(3);
     expect(onIndexChange).toHaveBeenCalledWith({ target: { value: 1 } });
   });

   it('passes the `index` state down as the `index` prop', () => {
     expect(wrapper.prop('index')).toBe(0);
     wrapper.setState({ index: 1 });
     expect(wrapper.prop('index')).toBe(1);
   });

   it('has an `index` state of 2 on decrement from 3', () => {
     wrapper.setState({ index: 3 });
     wrapper.prop('indexDecrement')();
     expect(wrapper.state('index')).toBe(2);
   });

   it('has an `index` state of 1 on increment', () => {
     wrapper.prop('indexIncrement')();
     expect(wrapper.state('index')).toBe(1);
   });

   it('has the max `index` state on decrement from 0', () => {
     wrapper.setState({ index: 0 });
     wrapper.prop('indexDecrement')(3);
     expect(wrapper.state('index')).toBe(2);
   });

   it('has the min `index` state on increment from the max', () => {
     wrapper.setState({ index: 2 });
     wrapper.prop('indexIncrement')(3);
     expect(wrapper.state('index')).toBe(0);
   });
 });
```

❶ It's standard for controllable components to provide a prop prefixed with default (not to be confused with a default prop) that allows the user to set the initial value without having to use the controlled pattern.

❷ This test shows the index prop in action, and how it always overwrites the internal state when set.

❸ Here we're testing that the component can switch back and forth between being controlled and uncontrolled. This is a common use case: the component consumer might want to "freeze" the slides until the user takes some action by setting slideIndex, then unset it to restore the normal slide behavior.

❹ This is another mock function test. expect(mockFunction).toHaveBeenCalledWith() makes an assertion about the most recent call to mockFunction. Notice that the expected argument to the change handler has the same shape as a DOM event; this is a standard convention in React.

Now you're ready to implement it:

```
ch5/src/HasIndex.js
import React from 'react';
import PropTypes from 'prop-types';

const capitalize = word => `${word[0].toUpperCase()}${word.slice(1)}`;

export default (Component, indexPropName) => {
  const defaultIndexPropName = `default${capitalize(indexPropName)}`;

  return class ComponentWithIndex extends React.PureComponent {
    static displayName = `HasIndex(${Component.displayName ||
      Component.name})`;

    static propTypes = {
      [indexPropName]: PropTypes.number,
      [defaultIndexPropName]: PropTypes.number,
      onIndexChange: PropTypes.func,
    };

    static defaultProps = {
      [defaultIndexPropName]: 0,
    };

    static getDerivedStateFromProps(props, state) {
      if (
        props[indexPropName] != null &&
        props[indexPropName] !== state.index
      ) {
        return { index: props[indexPropName] };
      }
      return null;
    }

    constructor(props) {
      super(props);

      this.state = {
        index: props[defaultIndexPropName],
      };
    }
```

```
      handleDecrement = upperBound => {
➤       const { onIndexChange } = this.props;
        this.setState(({ index }) => {
          const newIndex = upperBound
            ? (index + upperBound - 1) % upperBound
            : index - 1;
➤         if (onIndexChange) {
➤           onIndexChange({ target: { value: newIndex } });
➤         }
          return {
            index: newIndex,
          };
        });
      };

      handleIncrement = upperBound => {
➤       const { onIndexChange } = this.props;
        this.setState(({ index }) => {
          const newIndex = upperBound ? (index + 1) % upperBound : index + 1;
➤         if (onIndexChange) {
➤           onIndexChange({ target: { value: newIndex } });
➤         }
          return {
            index: newIndex,
          };
        });
      };

      render() {
➤       const {
➤         [defaultIndexPropName]: _defaultIndexProp,
➤         ...rest
➤       } = this.props;
➤       const indexProps = {
➤         [indexPropName]: this.state.index,
➤         [`${indexPropName}Decrement`]: this.handleDecrement,
➤         [`${indexPropName}Increment`]: this.handleIncrement,
➤       };
          return <Component {...rest} {...indexProps} />;
      }
    };
  };
```

❶ Since the index prop name is set at runtime, we need a bit of string manipulation to compute the name of its default-prefixed analogue. For example, the slideIndex prop will be accompanied by defaultSlideIndex.

❷ This code takes advantage of a new ES6 feature called "computed property names."[2] The expression inside of the square brackets is evaluated to determine the key.

❸ Added in React 16.3, getDerivedStateFromProps() is a lifecycle method called before every render. Here it's used to overwrite state.index with the index prop value when necessary. If no state changes are needed, it does nothing by returning null.

❹ Since the initial state is now derived from the initial props, we can no longer define it with the class property syntax. Instead we need to do so in a constructor. React constructors must call super(props), for reasons that are too esoteric to go into here.[3]

With that, Carousel is now controllable! Just to be sure, try adding a mount test to Carousel:

```
// src/tests/Carousel.test.js
import React from 'react';
import { mount, shallow } from 'enzyme';
import Carousel, { Carousel as CoreCarousel } from '../Carousel';
import CarouselButton from '../CarouselButton';
import CarouselSlide from '../CarouselSlide';

describe('Carousel', () => {
  ...
  describe('component with HOC', () => {
    ...
    it('allows `slideIndex` to be controlled', () => {
      const mounted = mount(<Carousel slides={slides} slideIndex={1} />);
      expect(mounted.find(CoreCarousel).prop('slideIndex')).toBe(1);
      mounted.setProps({ slideIndex: 0 });
      expect(mounted.find(CoreCarousel).prop('slideIndex')).toBe(0);
    });
    ...
  });
  ...
});
```

Commit your work:

```
:sparkles: Allow the index in HasIndex to be controlled
```

---

2. https://developer.mozilla.org/en-US/docs/Web/JavaScript/Reference/Operators/Object_initializer#Computed_property_names

3. https://overreacted.io/why-do-we-write-super-props/

Stacking Higher-Order Components

In React, a set of props can flow from one wrapper component to another to another, down a practically limitless chain, receiving modifications from each component. This creates infinite possibilities for combining HOCs. Extracting small pieces of functionality into HOCs, instead of allowing components to grow in complexity, is an important skill for keeping a React codebase manageable.

In this section, you'll add a new feature to Carousel: the ability to auto-advance the slideIndex on Carousel with a timer. All of the timer logic will be encapsulated in a new HOC.

Working with Timers

Let's create a new HOC called AutoAdvances. It'll be designed to work inside of a HasIndex, calling the increment function it receives after a certain time interval. The interval will be specified by a prop with a default value of, say, 10 seconds. The HOC should take two arguments, specifying which prop it should increment and which it should use to compute the upper bound for the increment function. The internal timer will reset every time the target prop (e.g., slideIndex) changes so that the carousel doesn't auto-advance immediately after the user switched slides using the "Prev" or "Next" buttons.

Start by creating a dummy implementation:

```
// src/AutoAdvances.js
import React from 'react';

export default (Component, propName, upperBoundPropName) =>
  class ComponentWithAutoAdvance extends React.PureComponent {
    static displayName = `AutoAdvances(${Component.displayName ||
      Component.name})`;

    render() {
      return <Component {...this.props} />;
    }
  };
```

Then formalize the HOC's requirements as a suite of tests. For the sake of brevity, all of the tests are presented at once below. If you're trying to practice TDD, you should add one test at a time, then modify the implementation to make that test pass before adding the next one:

```
ch5/src/tests/AutoAdvances.test.js
import React from 'react';
import { shallow } from 'enzyme';
import AutoAdvances from '../AutoAdvances';
```

```
describe('AutoAdvances()', () => {
  const MockComponent = () => null;
  MockComponent.displayName = 'MockComponent';
  const MockComponentWithAutoAdvance = AutoAdvances(
    MockComponent,
    'index',
    'upperBound'
  );

  it('has the expected displayName', () => {
    expect(MockComponentWithAutoAdvance.displayName).toBe(
      'AutoAdvances(MockComponent)'
    );
  });
```

❶
```
  const autoAdvanceDelay = 10e3;
  const upperBound = 5;
  let indexIncrement;
  let wrapper;
  beforeEach(() => {
    indexIncrement = jest.fn();
```
❷
```
    jest.useFakeTimers();
    wrapper = shallow(
      <MockComponentWithAutoAdvance
        autoAdvanceDelay={autoAdvanceDelay}
        index={0}
        indexIncrement={indexIncrement}
        upperBound={upperBound}
      />
    );
  });
```

```
  it('calls the increment function after `autoAdvanceDelay`', () => {
```
❸
```
    jest.advanceTimersByTime(autoAdvanceDelay);
    expect(indexIncrement).toHaveBeenCalledWith(upperBound);
  });

  it('uses `upperBound.length` if upperBound is an array', () => {
    wrapper.setProps({ upperBound: [1, 2, 3] });
    jest.advanceTimersByTime(autoAdvanceDelay);
    expect(indexIncrement).toHaveBeenCalledWith(3);
  });

  it('does not set a timer if `autoAdvanceDelay` is 0', () => {
    wrapper.setProps({ index: 1, autoAdvanceDelay: 0 });
    jest.advanceTimersByTime(999999);
    expect(indexIncrement).not.toHaveBeenCalled();
  });
```

```
  it('resets the timer when the target prop changes', () => {
    jest.advanceTimersByTime(autoAdvanceDelay - 1);
    wrapper.setProps({ index: 1 });
    jest.advanceTimersByTime(1);
    expect(indexIncrement).not.toHaveBeenCalled();
    jest.advanceTimersByTime(autoAdvanceDelay);
    expect(indexIncrement).toHaveBeenCalled();
  });

  it('clears the timer on unmount', () => {
    wrapper.unmount();
    jest.advanceTimersByTime(autoAdvanceDelay);
    expect(indexIncrement).not.toHaveBeenCalled();
  });
});
```

❶ 10e3 is scientific notation for 10 followed by 3 zeros, i.e. 10,000. This is a handy way to express the value "10 seconds" in milliseconds, the standard unit for timers in JavaScript.

❷ Using real timers would make our tests painfully slow, so Jest offers the ability to mock out the native timer functions with jest.useFakeTimers().[4] Calling it before each test ensures that the timer state is reset.

❸ When using fake timers, you need to manually "advance" them with jest.advanceTimersByTime(). For example, a simulated 10s timer will go off after one or more jest.advanceTimersByTime() calls adding up to a total of 10s.

❹ It's important to ensure that timers are cleaned up when components are unmounted. Enzyme's unmount() simulates this, invoking the component's componentWillUnmount() lifecycle method.

Now you have all the tests you need. Before you go on, you might want to brush up on React lifecycle methods.[5] This implementation will make use of componentDidMount(), componentDidUpdate(), and componentWillUnmount():

ch5/src/AutoAdvances.js
```
import React from 'react';
import PropTypes from 'prop-types';

export default (Component, propName, upperBoundPropName) =>
  class ComponentWithAutoAdvance extends React.PureComponent {
    static displayName = `AutoAdvances(${Component.displayName ||
      Component.name})`;
```

---

4.   https://jestjs.io/docs/en/timer-mocks.html
5.   https://reactjs.org/docs/react-component.html#commonly-used-lifecycle-methods

```
  static propTypes = {
    [propName]: PropTypes.number.isRequired,
    [`${propName}Increment`]: PropTypes.func.isRequired,
    [upperBoundPropName]: PropTypes.oneOfType([
      PropTypes.number,
      PropTypes.array,
    ]).isRequired,
    autoAdvanceDelay: PropTypes.number.isRequired,
  };

  static defaultProps = {
    autoAdvanceDelay: 10e3,
  };

  componentDidMount() {
    this.startTimer();
  }

  componentDidUpdate(prevProps) {
    if (
      prevProps[propName] !== this.props[propName] ||
      prevProps[upperBoundPropName] !== this.props[upperBoundPropName]
    ) {
      this.startTimer();
    }
  }

  componentWillUnmount() {
    clearTimeout(this._timer);
  }

  startTimer() {
    clearTimeout(this._timer);
    if (!this.props.autoAdvanceDelay) return;

    let upperBound;
    if (typeof this.props[upperBoundPropName] === 'number') {
      upperBound = this.props[upperBoundPropName];
    } else if (this.props[upperBoundPropName] != null) {
      upperBound = this.props[upperBoundPropName].length;
    }

    this._timer = setTimeout(() => {
      this.props[`${propName}Increment`](upperBound);
    }, this.props.autoAdvanceDelay);
  }

  render() {
    const { autoAdvanceDelay: _autoAdvanceDelay, ...rest } = this.props;
    return <Component {...rest} />;
  }
};
```

❶ The logic here compares the current value of the target prop to the previous value (that is, the value before the update that triggered componentDidUpdate()) and calls startTimer() if the value has changed. Likewise if the upper bound prop value has changed.

❷ When a component uses timers that should only fire if the component remains mounted, it should clear those timers in componentWillUnmount(). The underscore prefix for the timer handle, this._timeout, is a common convention for locally bound variables on component instances.

❸ Clearing any existing timer at the start of startTimer() ensures that only one timer is ever pending.

❹ Here, upperBound is allowed to be either a numeric value or the length of an array. In the case of Carousel, we know the upper bound will always be computed as slides.length, but allowing a number gives the HOC more flexibility.

Ready for a commit:

```
:sparkles: Add AutoAdvances HOC
```

Testing Multiple Higher-Order Components

Adding the new auto-advance functionality to Carousel should be a simple matter of importing the new AutoAdvances HOC and inserting it between the HasIndex wrapper and the core component:

ch5/src/Carousel.js
```
export default HasIndex(
  AutoAdvances(Carousel, 'slideIndex', 'slides'),
  'slideIndex'
);
```

But how do you use tests to confirm that all of these parts are wired together the way you expect? shallow() is ill-suited to this task. This calls for mount():

ch5/src/tests/Carousel.test.js
```
describe('component with HOC', () => {
  let mounted;

  beforeEach(() => {
    mounted = mount(<Carousel slides={slides} />);
  });

  it('passes `slides` down to the core component', () => {
    expect(mounted.find(CoreCarousel).prop('slides')).toBe(slides);
  });

  it('sets slideIndex={0} on the core component', () => {
    expect(mounted.find(CoreCarousel).prop('slideIndex')).toBe(0);
  });
```

```
  it('allows `slideIndex` to be controlled', () => {
    mounted = mount(<Carousel slides={slides} slideIndex={1} />);
    expect(mounted.find(CoreCarousel).prop('slideIndex')).toBe(1);
    mounted.setProps({ slideIndex: 0 });
    expect(mounted.find(CoreCarousel).prop('slideIndex')).toBe(0);
  });

  it('advances the slide after `autoAdvanceDelay` elapses', () => {
    jest.useFakeTimers();
    const autoAdvanceDelay = 10e3;
    mounted = mount(
      <Carousel slides={slides} autoAdvanceDelay={autoAdvanceDelay} />
    );
    jest.advanceTimersByTime(autoAdvanceDelay);
    mounted.update();
    expect(mounted.find(CoreCarousel).prop('slideIndex')).toBe(1);
  });
});
```

❶ One of the biggest "gotchas" in Enzyme's mount() is that a component's state changes don't cause its tree to re-render. So whenever you want to test that the mounted tree changes in response to some event, you'll need to manually call update().[6]

With those tests green, you can commit with confidence:

```
:sparkles: Add auto-advance support to Carousel
```

That concludes the coding portion of this chapter. You've successfully used HOCs for both refactoring and keeping new features in isolation, preventing complexity sprawl. Before the chapter concludes, we'll take a brief look at the components you've built from another angle.

Inspecting Components with React Devtools

Refactoring components into HOCs has the advantage of keeping code in manageable units, but as those units grow in number, it's easy to lose track of how they all fit together. One way to regain perspective is to take a look at the components in action through the React Developer Tools.[7]

Install the React Devtools in your browser of choice. Open the Carousel test page, then navigate to the React panel that the extension added to the developer console. You'll get a nice view of the entire tree of React components on the page, along with their props as shown in the screenshot on page 145.

---

6. https://airbnb.io/enzyme/docs/api/ReactWrapper/update.html
7. https://github.com/facebook/react-devtools

You can quickly locate any component you're interested in using the search bar. Click a component in the tree, and the selected component's props and state will appear on the right side. You can even edit (primitive) props and state values in real time and see what effects those changes have.

This bird's-eye view is invaluable for debugging. Start with the component that's rendering the unexpected output: most likely, the problem is caused by a problematic prop value. Work your way up the tree to see which component is passing that prop in. Then you can write up a unit test against that component to describe the problem, and quickly get it fixed.

Mantra: Keep the Unit Small

As applications grow in size, they grow more difficult for humans to understand as a whole. That's unavoidable. However, there's also a tendency for individual parts of the codebase to become more difficult to reconcile with one another, for indirect and implicit connections to be created that go unnoticed until they're accidentally corrupted, causing bugs. And that tendency is avoidable. You can be vigilant about keeping each module small enough for its purpose to come across clearly. In testing terms: *"Keep the unit small."*

In this chapter, you learned an important technique for keeping React components compact and purposeful: splitting layers of functionality into higher-order components (HOCs). You turned what could have been a single unwieldy component into three simple, reusable ones. And you learned to use the React Devtools to get a picture of how your components fit together to create an entire app.

With that, you have all the concepts you need to be a first-rate React developer. The next and final chapter will return to tooling, this time with the goal of improving collaboration.

CHAPTER 6

Continuous Integration and Collaboration

A recurring theme of this book has been the power of automation to improve your workflow. When properly applied, tools like ESLint and Jest greatly increase the chances that you'll catch mistakes in your code long before that code has a chance to go into production. But your workflow is just that: yours. When you're working as part of a team, or maintaining an open source project, how do you extend the power of automation to your collaborators?

One answer is good old-fashioned documentation: "Please run the tests before submitting a patch." But that leaves the door open for human error. A better solution is to offload such quality control checks to a server, away from the personalized environments of developer machines. This technique has become known as continuous integration (CI).

Continuous integration takes weight off of your shoulders as a project maintainer by allowing you to automate tasks you'd otherwise have to take on yourself. The CI server can tell potential contributors not only whether their patches pass the project's tests, but also how much those changes affect test coverage, compiled asset size, and any other metrics you care about.

Adding a CI server is a solid first step for project automation. You can go further by adding scripts to your contributors' development workflows and providing live documentation for developers to play with. Taking the time to set up all of these support tools will pay dividends by making your project's requirements crystal-clear to potential contributors and streamlining the process of reviewing their patches.

In this chapter, you'll learn to set up the popular Travis CI service to run the tests for the test-driven-carousel project. You'll also learn how to use Husky to add Git hooks to your project to check code before it's committed, spotting potential problems early. And finally, you'll generate sleek, interactive documentation for your carousel component with Storybook.

Setting Up Travis CI

Travis CI is a continuous integration service that's become enormously popular in recent years, thanks to its convenience and versatility. Travis can run your project's scripts automatically every time you or a collaborator pushes a change, and report the results through GitHub's "Pull Request" interface for branches. Each run is performed in its own isolated environment, producing more reliable results than you get in the personalized environment of a developer machine.

This section will walk you through the process of giving Travis CI access to your project, allowing you to offload tests and other automated tasks to the cloud. This will be a speedy process: You'll upload your project to GitHub, authorize Travis to access it, then add a configuration file to tell Travis to run your project's tests. Finally, you'll add a "badge" to show the world that your project's tests are passing on Travis CI.

Hosting Your Project on GitHub

Travis CI is designed as an extension of GitHub, the preeminent source code hosting giant. If you don't already have an account with GitHub, now would be a good time to create one.[1] Once you're logged in, create a new repository for your personal incarnation of the test-driven-carousel project. Be sure to make it a public repository: Travis CI is free for public, open source projects. You can ignore all of the other options as shown in the screenshot on page 149.

Once your repo is in place, GitHub will show you some command-line instructions for pushing an existing Git repository. Copy-and-paste those in the directory of the test-driven-carousel project from the last chapter:

```
$ git remote add origin git@github.com:TrevorBurnham/test-driven-carousel.git
$ git push -u origin master
Enumerating objects: 133, done.
Counting objects: 100% (133/133), done.
Delta compression using up to 8 threads
Compressing objects: 100% (130/130), done.
Writing objects: 100% (133/133), 289.48 KiB | 6.58 MiB/s, done.
Total 133 (delta 64), reused 0 (delta 0)
remote: Resolving deltas: 100% (64/64), done.
To github.com:TrevorBurnham/test-driven-carousel.git
 * [new branch]      master -> master
Branch 'master' set up to track remote branch 'master' from 'origin'.
```

---

1.   https://github.com/

Create a new repository

A repository contains all project files, including the revision history.

Owner   Repository name *

TrevorBurnham ▾   /   test-driven-carousel   ✓

Great repository names are short and memorable. Need inspiration? How about solid-barnacle?

Description (optional)

Carousel component project from the book Test-Driven React

◉ Public
   Anyone can see this repository. You choose who can commit.

○ Private
   You choose who can see and commit to this repository.

☐ Initialize this repository with a README
   This will let you immediately clone the repository to your computer. Skip this step if you're importing an existing
   repository.

Add .gitignore: None ▾   Add a license: None ▾   ⓘ

Create repository

Congratulations: your project is now hosted by GitHub! By default, that means that anyone who's interested in your project can not only download a copy, they can also suggest changes by submitting a *pull request*. When they do, you'll want to know whether your tests pass against their suggested changes. That's where Travis CI comes in.

Adding a Travis Configuration

Next, use your GitHub account to log in to Travis CI.[2] A screen will come up asking whether you want to grant the travis-pro organization access to your GitHub repositories. Authorize it—Travis needs that access to do its job. Once you're logged in, you may be prompted to activate another layer of GitHub integration, GitHub Apps. Allow that, too.

Once Travis is able to connect to your GitHub account, you'll see a list of your GitHub repositories, including test-driven-carousel. Click the link to the repo's

---

2.   https://travis-ci.com

Travis page. At this point, there isn't much to see, because Travis doesn't know what you want it to do for the project.

To change that, you'll need a file at the root of test-driven-carousel called .travis.yml. The .yml extension indicates that this is a YAML[3] file, which is a minimal human-readable syntax for data. Add a single entry:

ch6/.travis.yml
```
language: node_js
```

That's all Travis needs to recognize this as a Node project. One small problem: Travis defaults to an old version of Node, which will run into problems when trying to build test-driven-carousel. Fortunately, we can specify any Node version we want by adding a configuration file for nvm, the node version manager:[4]

ch6/.nvmrc
```
10.15
```

This tells Travis to switch to Node 10.15.x (the latest stable release as of this writing) before doing anything else.

Commit this modest addition:

```
:wrench: Add Travis CI and nvm configs
```

Then push to GitHub:

```
$ git push origin master
```

Now watch as the project's Travis page springs to life! Recognizing that test-driven-carousel is a Node project, it clones the project from GitHub, installs its dependencies from npm, then runs its tests for you:

```
> jest
 PASS  src/tests/Carousel.test.js
 PASS  src/tests/HasIndex.test.js
 PASS  src/tests/AutoAdvances.test.js
 PASS  src/tests/CarouselSlide.test.js
 PASS  src/tests/CarouselButton.test.js
Test Suites: 5 passed, 5 total
Tests:       35 passed, 35 total
Snapshots:   2 passed, 2 total
Time:        3.318s
Ran all test suites.
```

---

3. https://yaml.org
4. https://github.com/creationix/nvm

Pretty cool, right? Although you should run your tests before pushing any changes, it's reassuring to see the tests pass when another machine downloads your commit. And if anyone submits a pull request against your project, Travis will automatically run your tests against that branch and report the result there.

Adding a Status Badge

Let's add one final touch to our Travis integration. Right now, the result of Travis' latest test run is going to be tricky for anyone else to find. It's on a public but obscure Travis CI page. If your tests are passing, you should shout it from the rooftops! A common way to do that is to add a small image (known as a "badge") to the project README. Every time the badge loads, it shows the status of the latest build.

At the top of your project's Travis CI page, next to the project name, there should be a small image that says "build passing." That's the status badge. Click it to open a dialog where you can pick out an embeddable link. Choose "Markdown" from the format dropdown, then copy the little code snippet it generates.

Then create a REACT.md project in the root of your test-driven-carousel project. It's always a good idea for GitHub projects to have a README, since the README's contents are shown on the project's home page. Add a title, a short description, and the code you copied from Travis. The result should look something like this, with your GitHub username in place of username in the Build Status URLs:

```
ch6/README.md
# test-driven-carousel

[![Build Status](
  https://travis-ci.com/username/test-driven-carousel.svg?branch=master
)](https://travis-ci.com/username/test-driven-carousel)

Project from the book
[Test-Driven React](https://pragprog.com/book/tbreact/test-driven-react).
```

Save and commit using the suggested Gitmoji for documentation:

```
:memo: Add README with status badge
```

Then push:

```
$ git push origin master
```

Now your project's current build status will be displayed prominently on its GitHub page, as shown in the screenshot on page 152.

That's it for our coverage of Travis CI. There's lots more you can do with Travis—tests are only the beginning! Travis can do just about anything you can write a script for. For more information, check out the Travis CI docs.[5]

Git Hooks with Husky

If you followed along with Chapter 2, Integrated Tooling with VS Code, on page 17, you've adopted a cutting-edge development setup, completed with integrated linting and auto-formatting. However, your collaborators might not be so prepared. There's nothing stopping them from submitting a pull request that violates your project's prescribed ESLint or stylelint rules, or which will transform when you run it through Prettier. How can you enforce those rules? You could add checks to Travis CI, but then someone still has to fix the problems. Ideally, whoever introduced the problems should fix them *before* pushing their branch up for everyone else to see.

That's where Husky comes in. Husky is a tool for managing Git hooks in Java-Script projects. Git hooks are scripts that Git runs before or after certain commands, such as commit or push. In the olden days, developers had to install a project's Git hooks on their machine manually. Husky makes this much easier: when Husky is installed by npm (or yarn), it uses a post-install script[6] to install its own Git hooks, which will run whatever commands you specify for it in package.json. For developers working on your project, the process is effortless.

Be Considerate with Hooks

Git hooks are very powerful, and with great power comes great responsibility. Some project maintainers go overboard with hooks, forcing developers to run big, expensive scripts in the middle of their Git workflow. Respect your collaborators' time. If it takes more than a few seconds, maybe it should be a CI task rather than a Git hook.

---

5.   https://docs.travis-ci.com/
6.   https://docs.npmjs.com/misc/scripts

Setting Up Husky

Start by installing the husky package from npm:

```
$ npm install --save-dev husky@1.3.1
+ husky@1.3.1
```

Then add a new husky section to the project's package.json to specify the hooks. Start with just one, a pre-commit hook to run eslint .:

```
// package.json
...
"husky": {
  "hooks": {
    "pre-commit": "eslint ."
  }
},
...
```

Now try committing. Use the command line so you can see the full output:

```
$ git commit -a -m ":wrench: Add pre-commit ESLint check"
husky > pre-commit (node v8.12.0)
[master c8bcdab] :wrench: Add pre-commit ESLint check
 2 files changed, 79 insertions(+)
```

Since the linter was satisfied, there was no output from the pre-commit hook and the commit went through. If there had been any errors, you would've seen the ESLint output and the commit would have been blocked, giving you the chance to fix the problems and try committing again.

If you're ever in a situation where you need to skip a Git hook—for example, if you need help resolving the linter errors you're seeing, so you want to commit to a branch you can share with your colleagues—run the Git command with the --no-verify flag.

Chaining Checks

ESLint is just one of several tools you can run to check code before allowing a commit. Any command that returns an exit code (0 to indicate success, any other value for failure) will do the trick. The test-driven-carousel project already has three other tools available to run: stylelint, Prettier, and Jest. Running all of them before every commit could become cumbersome, though. Besides, Jest is already running on the CI. So let's stick to the linting/formatting trio.

Recall that we've already combined ESLint, Prettier, and stylelint in the lint script. So rather than duplicate the commands for those tools, we can run the existing script from the hook:

```
// package.json
...
"husky": {
  "hooks": {
    "pre-commit": "npm run lint"
  }
},
...
```

Give it a try:

```
$ git commit -a -m ":wrench: Add stylelint to pre-commit hook"
husky > pre-commit (node v8.12.0)

> test-driven-carousel@1.0.0 lint /Users/tburnham/code/test-driven-carousel
> npm run lint:js && npm run lint:css

> test-driven-carousel@1.0.0 lint:js /Users/tburnham/code/test-driven-carousel
> eslint . && prettier-eslint --list-different **/*.js

> test-driven-carousel@1.0.0 lint:css /Users/tburnham/code/test-driven-carousel
> stylelint **/*.js

[master d6fe670] :wrench: Add stylelint to pre-commit hook
1 file changed, 1 insertion(+), 1 deletion(-)
```

And we're set! With this precommit hook in place, everyone who works on this project will have a much easier time finding out whether they're following its formatting standards. Additionally, the same lint script would work perfectly on Travis CI, if you wanted to make it mark builds as bad when those scripts fail.

In a larger project, running all of these linters against the whole source tree before every commit could become cumbersome. If you run into that problem, you should check out lint-staged,[7] a package that allows you to run linters against only the files that are part of the pending commit.

Hopefully, you've gotten a hang of how you can use Husky to help developers identify and fix problematic code before they share it with the world. It's one of the simplest tools around, yet there's a ton you can do with it. To learn more, check out the Husky docs.[8]

Adding Docs with Storybook

Now that you're sharing our project with the world, you should think about taking the documentation to the next level. Storybook[9] has rapidly become a popular library for generating documentation pages for React components.

---

7. https://github.com/okonet/lint-staged
8. https://github.com/typicode/husky/blob/master/DOCS.md
9. https://storybook.js.org/

Using Storybook, you can integrate live examples with all the information devs need to take full advantage of your components.

Getting Started with Storybook

Storybook has a handy script that you can run with npx to get started:

```
$ npx -p @storybook/cli@4.1.11 sb init
```

Once that script finishes, you'll see that you have some new devDependencies:

```
// package.json
...
"devDependencies": {
  ...
  "@storybook/react": "^4.1.11",
  "@storybook/addon-actions": "^4.1.11",
  "@storybook/addon-links": "^4.1.11",
  "@storybook/addons": "^4.1.11"
},
...
```

And two new scripts:

```
// package.json
...
"scripts": {
  ...
  "storybook": "start-storybook -p 6006",
  "build-storybook": "build-storybook"
},
...
```

The script also added two new directories, .storybook and stories. The .storybook directory contains configuration, and the stories directory is where your documentation will live. The script generated some placeholder documentation in stories/index.stories.js.

Run the storybook script to start it up:

```
$ npm run storybook

Storybook 4.1.11 started
4.96 s for manager and 4.63 s for preview

Local:            http://localhost:6006/
On your network:  http://192.168.0.173:6006/
```

Under the hood, Storybook spun up a webpack server instance. Note that it's using its own built-in configuration, not the webpack.config.js from the project root.

Open the link to see the Storybook page. (In VS Code, you can open links shown in the integrated terminal using ⌘-click on macOS, ^-click on Windows and Linux.) You should see a nice welcome screen in your browser with a handy link to the Storybook documentation on writing stories.[10]

To see the Carousel component on this page, replace the placeholder documentation in stories.index.js with your own:

```
// stories/stories.index.js
import React from 'react';
import { storiesOf } from '@storybook/react';
➤ import Carousel from '../src/Carousel';
➤ import slides from '../example/slides';
➤
➤ storiesOf('Carousel', module).add('default', () => (
➤   <Carousel slides={slides} />
➤ ));
```

Moments after you save that, the change should immediately appear in the browser. Storybook's webpack server comes configured out of the box for hot module reloading (HMR), making updates very fast: the page receives the new JavaScript modules without having to refresh.

This is a good time for a commit:

```
:wrench: Initial Storybook setup
```

Now you have a Storybook page that shows Carousel in action. But if that's all there was to it, there wouldn't be much reason to use Storybook instead of the project's existing example server. So let's find out what else Storybook can do!

Enhancing Stories with Addons

The magic of Storybook is its extensibility, in the form of assorted addons.[11] There are abundant options for making your documentation richer through these handy plugins.

Let's start with the Actions addon. This will add a panel to the bottom of the page for reporting events. We'll use it to display onIndexChange events. Start by installing the addon from npm:

```
$ npm install --save-dev @storybook/addon-actions@4.1.11
+ @storybook/addon-actions@4.1.11
```

---

10. https://storybook.js.org/basics/writing-stories
11. https://storybook.js.org/addons/addon-gallery/

Then create a new file called .storybook/addons.js and add this line to register the new addon:

```
// .storybook/addons.js
import '@storybook/addon-actions/register';
```

The webpack server watches existing files for updates, but won't recognize new files, so you'll need to restart it before continuing.

Now add a bit of code to the Carousel story to tell the addon to listen for onIndex-Change:

```
// stories/index.stories.js
import React from 'react';
import { storiesOf } from '@storybook/react';
➤  import { action } from '@storybook/addon-actions';
import Carousel from '../src/Carousel';
import slides from '../example/slides';

storiesOf('Carousel', module).add('default', () => (
➤    <Carousel slides={slides} onIndexChange={action('onIndexChange')} />
));
```

With that change, you should see a new "Action Logger" panel at the bottom of the example page. Every time onIndexChange fires, either because you clicked the Prev/Next buttons or because the slides auto-advanced, the panel shows onIndexChange and the object that the listener received. It brings the API to life!

Let's try one more addon: Knobs. This one provides controls so that people can adjust the example's props directly from the page. We'll use it to make autoAdvanceDelay customizable. Install it from npm:

```
$ npm install --save-dev @storybook/addon-knobs@4.1.11
+ @storybook/addon-knobs@4.1.11
```

As with the Actions addon, Knobs requires you to register it:

```
ch6/.storybook/addons.js
import '@storybook/addon-actions/register';
➤  import '@storybook/addon-knobs/register';
```

Then use it to create a numeric control that sets the autoAdvanceDelay prop:

```
ch6/stories/index.stories.js
import React from 'react';
import { storiesOf } from '@storybook/react';
import { action } from '@storybook/addon-actions';
➤  import { withKnobs, number } from '@storybook/addon-knobs';
import Carousel from '../src/Carousel';
import slides from '../example/slides';

const stories = storiesOf('Carousel', module);
```

```
➤  stories.addDecorator(withKnobs);
   stories.add('default', () => (
➤    <Carousel
➤      autoAdvanceDelay={number('autoAdvanceDelay', 10e3)}
➤      slides={slides}
➤      onIndexChange={action('onIndexChange')}
➤    />
   ));
```

Now the page should have a second panel containing an input that you can use to change how quickly slides auto-advance, as shown in the following screenshot. Set it to 200 for a frenetic, 5-slides-per-second experience. Set it to 0 to disable it entirely.

Cool story, right? There's just one more thing we're going to do with it: publish!

Deploying to GitHub Pages

So far, we've been using Storybook in dev server mode. It's time to put the project's story on the web where the world can see it! Shut down the dev server, then make one change to package.json: add the args -o docs to the build-storybook script. This gives us our final package.json for the chapter:

ch6/package.json
```
{
  "name": "test-driven-carousel",
  "version": "1.0.0",
  "description": "",
  "main": "index.js",
  "scripts": {
    "test": "jest",
    "lint:js": "eslint . && prettier-eslint --list-different **/*.js",
    "lint:css": "stylelint **/*.js",
    "lint": "npm run lint:js && npm run lint:css",
    "format": "prettier-eslint --write **/*.js",
    "build": "webpack --config webpack.config.js",
    "dev": "webpack-dev-server --config webpack.config.js --open",
    "storybook": "start-storybook -p 6006",
    "build-storybook": "build-storybook -o docs"
  },
  "husky": {
    "hooks": {
      "pre-commit": "npm run lint"
    }
  },
  "keywords": [],
  "author": "",
  "license": "ISC",
  "devDependencies": {
    "@babel/core": "^7.1.2",
    "@babel/plugin-proposal-class-properties": "^7.1.0",
    "@babel/preset-env": "^7.1.0",
    "@babel/preset-react": "^7.0.0",
    "@storybook/addon-actions": "^4.1.11",
    "@storybook/addon-info": "^4.1.11",
    "@storybook/addon-knobs": "^4.1.11",
    "@storybook/addon-links": "^4.1.11",
    "@storybook/react": "^4.1.11",
    "babel-core": "7.0.0-bridge.0",
    "babel-eslint": "^10.0.1",
    "babel-jest": "^23.6.0",
    "babel-loader": "^8.0.4",
    "babel-plugin-styled-components": "^1.9.2",
    "enzyme": "^3.7.0",
    "enzyme-adapter-react-16": "^1.7.0",
    "enzyme-to-json": "^3.3.5",
    "eslint": "^5.1.0",
    "eslint-plugin-jest": "^21.17.0",
    "eslint-plugin-react": "^7.10.0",
    "html-webpack-plugin": "^3.2.0",
    "husky": "^1.3.1",
    "jest": "^23.6.0",
    "jest-styled-components": "^6.3.1",
```

```
  "prettier-eslint-cli": "^4.7.1",
  "stylelint": "^9.9.0",
  "stylelint-config-recommended": "^2.1.0",
  "stylelint-config-styled-components": "^0.1.1",
  "stylelint-processor-styled-components": "^1.5.1",
  "webpack": "^4.26.1",
  "webpack-cli": "^3.1.2",
  "webpack-dev-server": "^3.1.10"
},
"dependencies": {
  "prop-types": "^15.7.2",
  "react": "^16.4.2",
  "react-dom": "^16.4.2",
  "styled-components": "^4.1.1"
}
}
```

Like the dist directory, the docs directory is going to include some generated code that doesn't abide by our formatting standards, so add it to the project's .eslintignore and .prettierignore:

ch6/.eslintignore
```
dist/
➤ docs/
```

ch6/.prettierignore
```
dist/
➤ docs/
```

Now run the script:

```
$ npm run build-storybook
```

This will generate a static web version of the project's storybook in the docs directory we specified. (The particular choice of directory is important, for reasons that will become clear momentarily.) Once the script completes, create a commit with the new directory:

```
:memo: Build storybook docs
```

Then push that commit:

```
$ git push origin master
```

Now let's ask GitHub to host our new docs for us. Open the project's GitHub page and go to Settings. Scroll down to the "GitHub Pages" section. For the source, choose "master branch /docs folder," then click Save as shown in the screenshot on page 161.

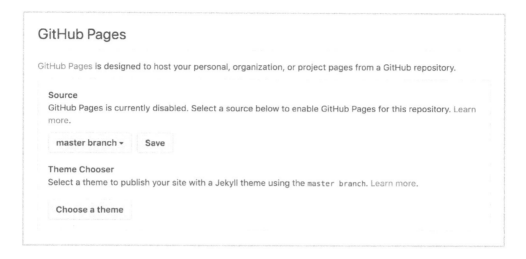

It may take a minute or two for GitHub to publish your page. You'll see a link from the project's Settings page to it. The address should be something like yourname.github.io/test-driven-carousel. Once it goes live, it should look exactly like your local Storybook page. Now every time you push changes to the docs directory on master, GitHub will update the project's documentation site.

As it is, this setup has one problem: if you make changes to the project but forget to run the build-storybook script, the docs will become stale. There are a couple of possible solutions to this. One possibility is to add a Husky hook to package.json, e.g.:

```
"husky": {
  "hooks": {
    "pre-push": "npm run build-storybook"
  }
},
```

That would be a bit of a nuisance for developers, who would have to wait on the build every time they commit a change. An ideal solution would be for Travis to take care of it. That requires a few extra steps. First, you'll want to go into the GitHub repo's settings and switch to using the gh-pages as the source of the docs; that will avoid the possibility of an infinite loop where Travis sees changes to master, rebuilds the docs, pushes the new docs to master, sees changes to master, etc. From there, follow Travis CI's guide to GitHub Pages deployment.[12]

---

12. https://docs.travis-ci.com/user/deployment/pages/

Mantra: Actively Automate

In the field of web development, bugs stemming from hardware failure are truly rare. If something goes awry, then in Hal 9000's famous words: "It must be human error." The task of building a bug-free website, then, is about minimizing human error. And with web-based applications growing ever more complex, we need all the help we can get. It's not enough to have good habits. If it can be done by software, software can do it more reliably than you can. So keep seeking out new ways to entrust development tasks to software. *"Actively automate."*

In this final chapter, we've gone through some of the tools that have arisen in the last few years to help JavaScript developers with common tasks like running tests, linting, and generating documentation. Although this was a brief tour, I hope you came away from it with a strong sense of how you can automate away many of the chores you'd otherwise have to deal with as a software project maintainer.

And that concludes our journey together. If you've developed a keener awareness of how your workflow impacts your work, then this book was a success. Because in the end, whether you're writing React components or any other kind of software, the path to becoming a better programmer is constant feedback. Treat every problem you run into as an opportunity to learn. Explore, experiment, play around. Never stop trying new things. Every expert started as a persistent novice.

Index

Thank you!

How did you enjoy this book? Please let us know. Take a moment and email us at support@pragprog.com with your feedback. Tell us your story and you could win free ebooks. Please use the subject line "Book Feedback."

Ready for your next great Pragmatic Bookshelf book? Come on over to https://pragprog.com and use the coupon code BUYANOTHER2019 to save 30% on your next ebook.

Void where prohibited, restricted, or otherwise unwelcome. Do not use ebooks near water. If rash persists, see a doctor. Doesn't apply to *The Pragmatic Programmer* ebook because it's older than the Pragmatic Bookshelf itself. Side effects may include increased knowledge and skill, increased marketability, and deep satisfaction. Increase dosage regularly.

And thank you for your continued support,

Andy Hunt, Publisher

SAVE 30%!
Use coupon code
BUYANOTHER2019

Practical Security

Most security professionals don't have the words "security" or "hacker" in their job title. Instead, as a developer or admin you often have to fit in security alongside your official responsibilities — building and maintaining computer systems. Implement the basics of good security now, and you'll have a solid foundation if you bring in a dedicated security staff later. Identify the weaknesses in your system, and defend against the attacks most likely to compromise your organization, without needing to become a trained security professional.

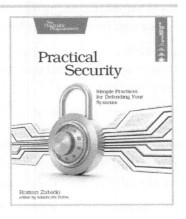

Roman Zabicki
(132 pages) ISBN: 9781680506341. $26.95
https://pragprog.com/book/rzsecur

Secure Your Node.js Web Application

Cyber-criminals have your web applications in their crosshairs. They search for and exploit common security mistakes in your web application to steal user data. Learn how you can secure your Node.js applications, database and web server to avoid these security holes. Discover the primary attack vectors against web applications, and implement security best practices and effective countermeasures. Coding securely will make you a stronger web developer and analyst, and you'll protect your users.

Karl Düüna
(230 pages) ISBN: 9781680500851. $36
https://pragprog.com/book/kdnodesec

Small, Sharp Software Tools

The command-line interface is making a comeback. That's because developers know that all the best features of your operating system are hidden behind a user interface designed to help average people use the computer. But you're not the average user, and the CLI is the most efficient way to get work done fast. Turn tedious chores into quick tasks: read and write files, manage complex directory hierarchies, perform network diagnostics, download files, work with APIs, and combine individual programs to create your own workflows. Put down that mouse, open the CLI, and take control of your software development environment.

Brian P. Hogan
(326 pages) ISBN: 9781680502961. $38.95
https://pragprog.com/book/bhcldev

iOS Unit Testing by Example

Fearlessly change the design of your iOS code with solid unit tests. Use Xcode's built-in test framework XCTest and Swift to get rapid feedback on all your code — including legacy code. Learn the tricks and techniques of testing all iOS code, especially view controllers (UIViewControllers), which are critical to iOS apps. Learn to isolate and replace dependencies in legacy code written without tests. Practice safe refactoring that makes these tests possible, and watch all your changes get verified quickly and automatically. Make even the boldest code changes with complete confidence.

Jon Reid
(300 pages) ISBN: 9781680506815. $47.95
https://pragprog.com/book/jrlegios

Web Development with ReasonML

ReasonML is a new, type-safe, functional language that compiles to efficient, readable JavaScript. ReasonML interoperates with existing JavaScript libraries and works especially well with React, one of the most popular front-end frameworks. Learn how to take advantage of the power of a functional language while keeping the flexibility of the whole JavaScript ecosystem. Move beyond theory and get things done faster and more reliably with ReasonML today.

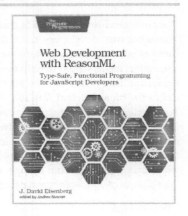

J. David Eisenberg
(206 pages) ISBN: 9781680506334. $45.95
https://pragprog.com/book/reasonml

Build Reactive Websites with RxJS

Upgrade your skill set, succeed at work, and above all, avoid the many headaches that come with modern front-end development. Simplify your codebase with hands-on examples pulled from real-life applications. Master the mysteries of asynchronous state management, detangle puzzling race conditions, and send spaceships soaring through the cosmos. When you finish this book, you'll be able to tame the wild code-beasts before they ever get a chance to wreck your day.

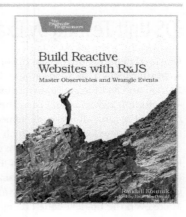

Randall Koutnik
(194 pages) ISBN: 9781680502954. $38.95
https://pragprog.com/book/rkrxjs

Rediscovering JavaScript

JavaScript is no longer to be feared or loathed—the world's most popular and ubiquitous language has evolved into a respectable language. Whether you're writing frontend applications or server-side code, the phenomenal features from ES6 and beyond—like the rest operator, generators, destructuring, object literals, arrow functions, modern classes, promises, async, and metaprogramming capabilities—will get you excited and eager to program with JavaScript. You've found the right book to get started quickly and dive deep into the essence of modern JavaScript. Learn practical tips to apply the elegant parts of the language and the gotchas to avoid.

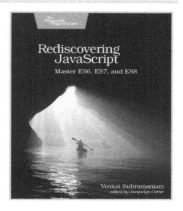

Venkat Subramaniam
(286 pages) ISBN: 9781680505467. $45.95
https://pragprog.com/book/ves6

Simplifying JavaScript

The best modern JavaScript is simple, readable, and predictable. Learn to write modern JavaScript not by memorizing a list of new syntax, but with practical examples of how syntax changes can make code more expressive. Starting from variable declarations that communicate intention clearly, see how modern principles can improve all parts of code. Incorporate ideas with curried functions, array methods, classes, and more to create code that does more with less while yielding fewer bugs.

Joe Morgan
(282 pages) ISBN: 9781680502886. $47.95
https://pragprog.com/book/es6tips

The Pragmatic Bookshelf

The Pragmatic Bookshelf features books written by developers for developers. The titles continue the well-known Pragmatic Programmer style and continue to garner awards and rave reviews. As development gets more and more difficult, the Pragmatic Programmers will be there with more titles and products to help you stay on top of your game.

Visit Us Online

This Book's Home Page
https://pragprog.com/book/tbreact
Source code from this book, errata, and other resources. Come give us feedback, too!

Keep Up to Date
https://pragprog.com
Join our announcement mailing list (low volume) or follow us on twitter @pragprog for new titles, sales, coupons, hot tips, and more.

New and Noteworthy
https://pragprog.com/news
Check out the latest pragmatic developments, new titles and other offerings.

Save on the eBook

Save on the eBook versions of this title. Owning the paper version of this book entitles you to purchase the electronic versions at a terrific discount.

PDFs are great for carrying around on your laptop—they are hyperlinked, have color, and are fully searchable. Most titles are also available for the iPhone and iPod touch, Amazon Kindle, and other popular e-book readers.

Buy now at *https://pragprog.com/coupon*

Contact Us

Online Orders: *https://pragprog.com/catalog*
Customer Service: *support@pragprog.com*
International Rights: *translations@pragprog.com*
Academic Use: *academic@pragprog.com*
Write for Us: *http://write-for-us.pragprog.com*
Or Call: +1 800-699-7764

Lightning Source UK Ltd.
Milton Keynes UK
UKHW030623060619
343937UK00003B/22/P